Testimonials

As a former English teacher, I can tell you that students, from elementary school on through Advanced Placement English, need a structured study of grammar. Dr. Roach's meticulous research and clear curriculum guidance provide a much needed resource for today's ELA teacher. With proven results, Dr. Roach's approach to grammar is sure to improve knowledge—and high stakes test scores—for teachers and students who use it.

—Dr. Lienne F. Medford, Dean of the Graduate School and Professor of Leadership, Converse University

Dr. Roach and I worked in the same South Carolina school district but in different middle schools. Our district had just introduced the EVAAS teacher evaluation system ranking teacher effectiveness from a level 1(lease effective) to a level 5 (most effective). At Christmas break that year, I calculated my score and discovered that I was a level 2 teacher. Needless to say, I was devastated and cried the entire holiday. Upon speaking with Dr. Roach, she invited me to begin planning with her, and I gladly took her up on the offer. While I did make a few changes in how and what I taught, the biggest change was that I began using her method of teaching grammar in a systematic way. By the end of that school year, and much to my surprised elation, I was an EVAAS level 5 teacher. I have seen such success each year, and I will never go back to teaching any other way!

—Dr. Wanda Cody, Former Middle School English Language Arts Teacher and Current College English Professor

Around my 20th year in the classroom and after multiple attempts at teaching grammar effectively and being unsuccessful in having the skills transfer to student writing, I had the unique privilege of working alongside Dr. Roach during the development stage of this book. This firsthand experience allowed me to see the methodologies in action as they were being refined and perfected. Dr. Roach personally guided me through the techniques presented in the book, giving me invaluable insights into their practical application and effectiveness. This book's systematic approach to grammar instruction is nothing short of transformative. It breaks down complex grammatical concepts into digestible chunks, allowing teachers like myself to grasp the underlying structure of the English language. More importantly, it provides a clear roadmap for translating this understanding into effective teaching strategies.

—Mrs. Michelle Hydrick,
Secondary English Teacher

Dr. Roach mentored me as a new teacher whose students were struggling with grammar. I had one of my toughest groups of students that year, and she coached me on how to teach grammar systematically and intentionally. My students' growth that year was exponential in grammar and across the board. I still use her methods today and continue to see growth. I highly recommend her teaching methods!

—Ms. Lauren Rodriguez, Middle School English
Language Arts Teacher

Getting the Gist of the English Language

Using Systematic Grammar Instruction to Improve the Teaching and Learning of Writing

Jennifer Roach, Ed.D.

Edited by: Molly A. Isaacs-McLeod
Interior design: The Printed Page
Cover design: The Printed Page

Published by
Gifted Unlimited, LLC
12340 U.S. Highway 42, No. 453
Goshen, KY 40026
www.giftedunlimitedllc.com

ISBN: 978-1-953360-35-9

Printed and bound in the United States of America.

Table of Contents

Acknowledgements

I am deeply grateful to Michael Clay Thompson for his invaluable contributions to the field of grammar. His work has not only deepened my own understanding but has both transformed my approach to teaching and inspired much of the research behind this book. I also extend my sincere appreciation to Dean Lienne F. Medford, Dr. Jeffery S. Martin, and Dr. Keshia Jackson Gilliam, all of Converse University, for their unwavering belief in and support of my research. Thank you to Dr. Michael Cory, formerly of Gettys Middle School, for seeing my potential as both a teacher and a leader and for giving me the autonomy to practice these methods. Thank you to my dad, Bill Cody, for instilling in me that anything worth doing is worth doing right. Thank you to my mom, Wanda Cody, for showing me how to be a lifelong learner as we have studied and taught together. Thank you to my son, Colton Hoover, who grew up alongside me as I pursued my education and began my teaching career. Thank you to my husband, Kevin Roach, for supporting me in achieving all of my dreams. Thank you to the rest of my beloved family whose names are represented on the cover of this book. Finally, thank you to all of the students and teachers who have shaped me as an educator.

THE PAST

Chapter 1
Problems Caused by the Anti-Grammar Movement

Five Problems Caused by the Anti-Grammar Movement

Teaching grammar does not currently have widespread support in education, and there seems to be a bias against the practice in most of the educational research available. In fact, teaching grammar has been taboo for the last several decades in public education. Many school districts view grammar as a bad word; therefore, grammar teaching is not usually found on any list of best teaching practices. "Some school systems forbid the teaching of grammar, and teachers get bad evaluations if they violate the prohibition."[1] Part of the problem is that teachers and even some educational leaders were never taught the foundations of the language, and now, they do not feel comfortable teaching it to students. There has been a pervasive belief that students will "pick up" on the rules of grammar by being exposed to good writing, but what about students who come from homes where they are not exposed to good writing? "What about these students, typically low income, with few books at home, who struggle to move from reading a gorgeous sentence to knowing how to write one? Could there be a better, less soul-crushing way to enforce the basics?"[2] Furthermore, even for those students that are read to from birth, what has become the common approach to teaching grammar, or at times not teaching it at all, is not working! "Freewriting, hoping that children will learn or gain a love of writing, hasn't worked."[3]

The term Anti-Grammar Movement includes researchers such as Braddock (1963), Lloyd-Jones (1963), Schoer (1963), Weaver (1979), Krashen (1987), and Noguchi (1991) whose work has supported either the removal of grammar teaching altogether or the limiting of teaching grammar in a systematic way. In her work, Constance Weaver "argues that the traditional definition and terms, especially parts of speech, are not useful or entirely truthful."[4] As a result of these influences, "many educators are concerned less with sentence-level mechanics than with helping students draw inspiration from their own lives and from literature."[5] This movement has resulted in several problems that plague American public education.

Problem 1: Conflicting Viewpoints

Views among educational leaders and researchers concerning grammar teaching remain polarized. Some leaders believe systematic, direct instruction in grammar is an effective practice; some believe that grammar teaching should only happen within the context of student writing, yet others believe that any grammar teaching at all is ineffective. Because of these differing philosophies, educational leaders are giving mixed messages to teachers concerning the teaching of grammar. One teacher commented in his Master's Diploma Thesis that he had a choice to make—"to follow either the example of the teachers who [he] had observed at school or the model presented to [him] at Masaryk University during [his] studies."[6] This teacher is not alone; many teacher preparation programs are encouraging new teachers to avoid teaching grammar, and if programs advocate teaching it at all, it is only to teach it in the context of student writing. An article called "Why Kids Can't Write" published in the New York Times reported on this issue.

> According to Kate Walsh, president of the National Council on Teacher Quality, a scan of course syllabuses from 2,400 teacher preparation programs turned up little evidence that the teaching of writing was being covered in a widespread or systematic way. A separate 2016 study of nearly 500 teachers in grades three through eight across the country, conducted by Gary Troia of Michigan State University and Steve Graham of Arizona State University, found that fewer than half had taken a college class that devoted significant time to the teaching of writing, while fewer than a third had taken a class solely devoted to how children learn to write.[7]

Despite the lack of proper training, practicing teachers are realizing that there are several problems with abiding by the research that promotes only teaching grammar in context. One teacher stated that she felt "caught between conviction that students need to be able to use the patterns and conventions of written English and awareness of the research."[8] This teacher's statement shows how "teaching pedagogy and public expectation stand at odds."[9] As a result, some teachers comply and do not spend time teaching grammar in isolation or as a system even if they think that students would benefit from it. Other teachers choose to ignore the research and do what they believe to be best for students. This often creates a discrepancy in what teachers are told about teaching grammar. This problem extends beyond teacher preparation programs. First-year teachers are often encouraged to shun grammar teaching by district-level leadership, but then they are encouraged to embrace it by some highly successful veteran teachers.

Early in my teaching career, I found myself in the same position. I taught using Nancy Atwell's writing workshop model, was passionate about having students write about their lives, and spent time conferencing with each individual student about his or her work. I would "cherry-pick" my mini-lessons based on student writing conferences. For example, if I found that a student was struggling with commas between coordinate adjectives, I would either discuss it with him or her individually or add in a mini-lesson on that topic the following week. However, I became increasingly frustrated because I was constantly circling back to the same concepts without seeing any mastery or improvement in my students' writing. They would fix mistakes but often could neither explain why errors were made nor identify solutions to help avoid similar issues in the future. At the time, the Instructional Coach in my school was adamantly opposed to both teaching grammar in isolation and to spending any considerable amount of instructional time on it, period. She mandated that any grammar instruction take place through individual or small group conferences. However, the Gifted and Talented Coordinator for the district had a different view and supported teaching grammar in a systematic way. I was confronted with mixed messages between school leadership and district leadership and realized that I needed to make a choice by forming my own opinion. In the midst of this dilemma, I developed the desire to uncover the best way to teach grammar to students. I grew a personal interest in finally putting the great grammar debate to rest. Later that year, I attended a professional development presented by Michael Clay Thompson, and this one-day session reshaped my pedagogy and transformed my teaching practices. For the first time, all of the facts that I knew about the structure of the English language began to fit together in my mind into a system that could be used to transform writing.

Michael Clay Thompson is an acclaimed speaker, an educational consultant, and the author of over 100 books published by Royal Fireworks Press. Michael Clay Thompson's approach to grammar instruction hinges on the fact that students must have prior knowledge of grammar concepts before they can effectively produce academic writing. Therefore, "four-level grammar must precede the instruction of academic writing."[10] Thompson's four-level approach includes teaching grammar as a complex system made up of four levels that build on one another—the parts of speech, the parts of the sentence, phrases, and clauses. After adopting this approach, I began to see my own students' writing abilities and test scores soar. In addition, my colleagues who began to teach this way saw their own students succeed in the same ways.

Despite the success that both my students and some of my colleagues began to experience, I was still often met with resistance from both teachers and educational leaders concerning the teaching of grammar. While serving as a mentor for a new teacher, the teacher explained that she wanted to follow my advice but was worried to do so because not everyone agreed. She brought to my attention that someone in a district-level position announced to all of the first-year English teachers that they should not waste time teaching grammar.

Because of the conflicting recommendations of whether or not to teach grammar and how to teach it, many teachers have begun to assume omitting direct grammar instruction from their classrooms is at least considered acceptable practice and in extreme cases considered best practice. "These assumptions are reinforced by journal articles that reject formal grammar instruction. The dismissal of grammar teaching is unfortunate not only because practice has shown that teachers must know grammar to analyze student errors but also because many questions regarding grammar instruction are worth studying."[11]

Problem 2: The Anti-Grammar Movement Based Conclusions on Faulty Research

Teachers and educational leaders began to scorn the idea of teaching grammar due to research dating back to the 1960s and 1970s. One of the most popular studies that the anti-grammar movement cites is from the work of Braddock, Lloyd-Jones, and Schoer. The study stated, "The teaching of formal grammar has a negligible or, because it usually displaces some instruction and practice in composition, even a harmful effect on the improvement of writing."[12] However, those who interpret this quote to mean that all grammar instruction is a waste of time usually fail to mention the passage that precedes it: "Uncommon, however, is carefully conducted research which studies composition over an extended period of time."[13] It is clear that the researchers, Braddock, Lloyd-Jones, and Schoer, admitted that there were limitations to their study, and the fact that students were not studied over a longer period is a huge concern. After all, it takes time for students to learn grammar as a system and be able to translate that to writing.

In addition to the issue of time, Meckel's research in the 1960s points out two other faulty areas concerning the research conducted by Braddock, Lloyd-Jones, and Schoer:

> First, none of the grammar studies up to 1963 extended beyond one semester—'a time span much too short to permit development of the degree of conceptualization necessary for transfer to take place.' Second, none of the studies had to do with editing and revising, that is 'with situations in which pupils are recasting the structure of a sentence or a paragraph.' Finally, none of the studies makes comparisons between students who had demonstrated a knowledge of grammar and those of equal intelligence who had none.[14]

Another popular study cited by the anti-grammar movement was conducted in the 1970s by John Mellon and Frank O'Hare. They claimed that students can learn grammar simply by writing and without any direct instruction in grammar topics. However, this claim was later discredited by O'Hare's own subsequent publication. He published The Modern Writer's Handbook in 1993, and a large portion of this book contains very traditional grammar. "If O'Hare doesn't believe in the validity of his own study, why should anyone else?"[15] Furthermore, why would writers need a handbook instructing them in grammar rules if direct instruction is unnecessary?

Current practitioners find many problems with the idea that grammar improves simply because of more writing and disagree with the notion that students who write more just naturally grow to make fewer errors. Instead, this result could simply indicate "that the students who don't trip over grammatical problems tend to write more; it says nothing about those students who write less and do have problems—and they are the ones who need help."[16] The belief that students will learn correct Standard English through the osmosis of complex texts that they read and write is based on the faulty assumption that all students have access to extensive resources for reading and writing, and unfortunately, teachers know that simply is not true.

Michael Clay Thompson points out that "direct instruction in grammar has been deplored by whole-language dicta that forbid anything being taught in isolation. [However,] the injunction not to teach anything in isolation must be weighed against the probability that essential knowledge will not be taught at all."[17] Unfortunately, this probability has become a reality, and grammar has in many cases not been taught at all. Thompson continues, "Many things, such as mathematics and Latin, are effectively taught in isolation, and it is difficult to grasp why crucial intellectual components such as grammar, with its system of interlocking subsystems, are harmed by focus."[18] An understanding of the system of the English language can do nothing but improve students' abilities to read and write that language.

Problem 3: The Drastic Decline in American Literacy

A report to Carnegie Corporation of New York entitled Writing Next: Effective Strategies to Improve Writing of Adolescents in Middle and High Schools warns, "American students today are not meeting even basic writing standards, and their teachers are at a loss for how to help them. In an age overwhelmed by information...we should view this as a crisis, because the ability to read, comprehend, and write—in other words, to organize information into knowledge—can be viewed as tantamount to a survival skill."[19] The literacy crisis in the United States is evidenced by the following statistics:

- More than 30 million adults in the United States cannot read, write, or do basic math above a third-grade level. —ProLiteracy
- Children whose parents have low literacy levels have a 72 percent chance of being at the lowest reading levels themselves. These children are more likely to get poor grades, display behavioral problems, have high absentee rates, repeat school years, or drop out. —National Bureau of Economic Research (NBER)
- 75 percent of state prison inmates did not complete high school or can be classified as low literate. —Rand Report: Evaluating the Effectiveness of Correctional Education[20]

Problem 4: The Regression of Academic Writing Ability

Academic writing refers to the type of writing required in high school or college classes and to the type of writing required in professional settings. Johnson (2016) defines academic writing as "the types of writing used in college-level writing courses."[21] Whereas creative writing focuses on voice and word choice, academic writing focuses on content/ideas, organization, and grammatical correctness. Michael Clay Thompson (2009) suggests that academic writing must be "in standard academic English, in organized essay structure, with correct grammar, spelling, and punctuation. The academic genre is the most important, and it must dominate [educators'] priorities."[22]

One main problem with the anti-grammar movement is that "with the advent of the Communicative Approach in [English Language Teaching], grammar has been marginalized as the focus has shifted from accuracy to communicative competence. Yet, an obvious decline in written proficiency has been noticed due basically to poor grammar."[23] The National Assessment of Educational Progress (NAEP)—"also known as The Nation's Report Card—showed that more than 75% of students at grades 8 and 12 performed at or above the Basic achievement level, meaning that they have at least partial mastery of the knowledge and skills needed to communicate clearly in writing. But only about a quarter of the 8th and 12th graders wrote at or above the Proficient level, which means they demonstrate solid academic performance."[24] This means that only roughly 25% of America's eighth and twelfth graders are proficient in writing.[25] One report states:

> Writing well is not just an option for young people—it is a necessity. Along with reading comprehension, writing skill is a predictor of academic success and a basic requirement for participation in civic life and in the global economy. Yet every year in the United States large numbers of adolescents graduate from high school unable to write at the basic levels required by colleges or employers. In addition, every school day 7,000 young people drop out of high school (Alliance for Excellent Education, 2006), many of them because they lack the basic literacy skills to meet the growing demands of the high school curriculum (Kamil, 2003; Snow & Biancarosa, 2003). Because the definition of literacy includes both reading and writing skills, poor writing proficiency should be recognized as an intrinsic part of this national literacy crisis.[26]

Many educators blame students' lack of ability to adhere to Standard English in their writing on the digital generation of social media. "After all, the Snapchat generation may produce more writing than any group of teenagers before it, writing copious text messages and social media posts, but when it comes to the formal writing expected at school and work, they struggle with the mechanics of simple sentences."[27] Maybe the real problem is that students "were never taught how to think and write properly."[28] Thompson suggests that grammar is a "high form of critical thinking about language."[29] This ability to think about the English language is an important skill as evidenced by its inclusion on the ACT. "The ACT includes measures of five distinct academic skills: English, math, reading, science, and writing."[30] Two of these five skills, both English and writing, are impacted by having a working knowledge of the structure of the English language. This is further evidenced by the fact that ACT writing is scored in four domains: ideas and analysis, development and support, organization, and most relevant to this study, language use and conventions.[31]

What can public school teachers do about this crisis? NAEP showed that "the average writing score for grade 8 students attending public schools was 16 points lower than the average score for students attending private schools, and 18 points lower than students in Catholic schools."[32] "Teachers who argue against teaching grammar are, in fact, limiting the writing of many students to recreational use only. How often do English teachers say, 'they write fine when we're doing narratives, but when we get to expository writing, everything falls apart'? 'Everything' usually includes grammar."[33] One educator gave his expert opinion on the deficiency in student writing, "'My students can't write a clear sentence to save their lives, and I've had it,' Joseph R. Teller, an English professor at College of the Sequoias, wrote in the Chronicle of Higher Education."[34] This inability to produce academic writing negatively affects students beyond the K-12 classroom and follows them into college and their careers.

The decline in students' academic writing skills has been rapid. "Annual reports from the National Center for Education Statistics show that the SAT mean scores in writing have dropped from 497 to 484 in 9 years (2006-2015). It's already bad that the score is decreasing, but it also never stayed the same two years in a row during this period. Therefore, we can assume that the SAT result in writing will continue to decrease at the same rate."[35] One article entitled, "Why Kids Can't Write," published in The New York Times reported that according to the data from NAEP, "40 percent of those who took the ACT writing exam in the high school class of 2016 lacked the reading and writing skills necessary to complete successfully a college-level English compositional class."[36] The ACT National Profile Report of the Graduation Class of 2018 (2018) shows that the percent of students who met college readiness benchmarks in English has steadily decreased from 64% in 2014, to 61% in 2016, and now to 60% in 2018.[37] The report later states that only one-half of all high school graduates who took the ACT Writing test met the national benchmark and showed college readiness.[38] Keep in mind that this result only takes into account students who believed themselves to be college-bound and therefore took the ACT. It does not account for the students being educated in our public schools that are not pursuing college. Preparing half of the students interested in college to get there is not acceptable!

This deficiency in writing skills is also spilling over into the workplace. In an article from The Washington Post, the author states, "According to national surveys, employers want to hire college graduates who can write coherently, think creatively and analyze quantitative data. But the Conference Board has found in its surveys of corporate hiring leaders that writing skill is one of the biggest gaps in workplace readiness."[39] The article goes on to explain, "Writing and communications are the most requested job requirements across nearly every industry."[40] Another study agrees, "A wide range of jobs require employees to produce written documentation, visual/text presentations, memoranda, technical reports, and electronic messages. The explosion of electronic and wireless communication in everyday life brings writing skill into play as never before."[41] However, the lack of writing proficiency among employees has become "critical in the workplace and…directly affects hiring and promotion decisions. The demand for writing proficiency is not limited to professional jobs but extends to clerical and support positions in government, construction, manufacturing, service industries, and elsewhere."[42] Clearly, this problem is affecting society negatively because the American public school system is not truly producing college and career-ready students. Michael Clay Thompson suggests, "Prescriptive grammar instruction is correct. There are, in fact, language standards in the professional world that students will be expected to observe, and it is [a] disservice to these students to [fail to] prepare them to meet such standards."[43]

Problem 5: The "Dumbing Down" of English Language Arts Curriculum Resulting in Students Not Being Able to Think about Language

One of the reasons that teachers agreed to remove grammar from the curriculum is because many students and teachers viewed grammar as boring, tedious, complicated, and hard. Teachers and students were tired of grammar worksheets and diagramming sentences. Michael Clay Thompson asserts, "American education has largely discarded…traditional grammar, which is thought to be unteachable, unlearnable, unlikable, useless, remedial, and inappropriate."[44]

However, grammar is simply a way of thinking about the system of a language. "Grammar gives kids a way to think about language, to see what language reveals about their own minds, to think about how language makes clarity, to think about how different authors use language in their own styles, to think about crafting the language of their own sentences."[45] It becomes a "magic lens that reveals amazing things."[46] Grammar allows students to analyze the parts of speech, the parts of the sentence, phrases, and clauses in order to see how they fit together as a complex system. That system works together to form solid, academic writing.

Removing something from teaching and learning simply because it can be difficult is never what is best for students. What if math teachers stopped teaching algebra simply because it is difficult? What if science teachers stopped teaching the scientific method simply because students struggle with it? While these examples may sound absurd, this is exactly what happened concerning grammar teaching in the English Language Arts curriculum. Professor Carl Singleton argues, "I know research exists that purports to prove that there is no connection between basic skills in English and the ability to write well. Such research must be flawed. It is impossible to write good English without those skills. Students cannot learn to write until they have mastered the basics, any more than they can learn calculus before algebra and trigonometry or particle theory before beginning physics. To believe otherwise is to waste vast amounts of time, energy, and money."[47]

Rather than removing grammar instruction completely, a better approach would be to find ways to make learning and applying grammar exciting and relevant for students. Michael Clay Thompson argues, "The negative stereotype of grammar as a tedious waste of time should be rejected. Students must attack grammar with enthusiasm in order to use it as a high form of critical thinking about language. This will produce self-knowledge, appreciation of literature, and an ability to enjoy making good sentences and compositions."[48] Kelly Gallagher (1975) "urged educators to go beyond 'sterile presentation of grammar and syntax.'"[49] Thompson suggests that not only can grammar be successfully taught but also that grammar is full of "symmetries and mysteries enough to fascinate the dullest mind, and is an introspective and metacognitive way of thinking about our own ideas."[50] Thompson encourages teachers with the following advice: "It is easy to forget, when looking at a ponderous grammar textbook, what a tiny topic grammar is. The total number of terms necessary to acquire useful fundamentals of traditional grammar is about 50. There are only eight parts of speech, about five parts of the sentence, several kinds of phrases, and a few clauses."[51] Grammar is both teachable and learnable!

No child ever rises to low expectations, yet there continues to be a push to limit the teaching and learning of English grammar.

No child ever rises to low expectations, yet there continues to be a push to limit the teaching and learning of English grammar. Systematic grammar instruction has a profound impact on students' abilities to engage in academic writing. "The first step in mastering any field is gaining an overview of its structure, which requires classification of its elements."[52] In order to master academic writing, students must first master the structure of the English language.

Chapter 2

Reflecting on the Past: The Historical Context of Grammar Teaching

Every language has a grammatical structure. The term, "grammar" itself traces back to a Greek word "grammatika" or "grammatike techne" which was translated as the art of writing.[53] "Like other sciences that the Greeks developed, grammar was not invented to enable them to do something, but to do something better, with conscious control. As bronze armor made them better warriors, so grammar enabled them to understand poetry better, appreciate its artistry, catalog the peculiarities of ancient dialects, analyze meters, correct scribal errors in manuscripts, recognize interpolations, assign authorship to anonymous fragments, and so forth—in short, to practice philology [the branch of knowledge that deals with the structure, historical development, and relationships of a language or languages]."[54] The very history of the word grammar itself proves its value in its ability to enhance the art of writing.

"Throughout the development of western civilization, beginning in the Hellenistic period, grammar has normally been viewed as the essential academic discipline on which all others are based."[55] "During the Middle Ages, grammar was considered the foundation of all knowledge, the necessary prerequisite for understanding theology and philosophy as well as literature. Author Jeffrey F. Huntsman (1983) explained, "Grammar was thought to discipline the mind and the soul at the same time."[56]

"By the nineteenth century, the prominent approach to teaching English was the grammar-translation method (GTM) which had its roots in the teaching of Latin. The goal was not primarily to develop the ability to communicate, but to learn the grammatical system. Grammar was taught deductively through the presentation and study of grammar rules, which the students then practiced through translation exercise. It was also taught in a systematic and sequenced way, using the students' L1 for grammar instruction."[57] L1 refers to a speaker's first language, so traditionally as students learned their native language, they also studied the system and structure of that language.

In the United States during the 1950s, "The study of the English language was an important part of every school day. Every student took four years of English, and half of each year was devoted to the study of grammar, syntax, spelling, punctuation, and speech. The other half was reserved for the study of literature."[58] Teachers in every content area expected their students to write English correctly and corrected student work for both spelling and grammar mistakes.

For the last half-century, many educators have believed that they "have justifiable reasons for erasing formal grammar instruction from their composition classrooms. The Braddock Report of 1963—Research in Written Composition (Braddock, Lloyd-Jones, and Schoer, 1963)—and similar studies since then have told [them] that formal grammar instruction not only does not improve [their] students' writing but in fact may have an adverse effect on their compositions. Such studies…have placed audience, purpose, and politics in the writing classroom well above grammar."[59] Out of this research, the anti-grammar movement grew.

Progressive Education versus Traditional Grammar Teaching

"It was not until the beginning of the twentieth century in America that a full-fledged revolt against the liberal arts occurred. This happened under the banner of 'progressive education'"[60] and resulted in the "elimination of formal instruction in grammar."[61] Constance Weaver, an opponent of systematic grammar teaching, points out in her article, "Teaching Grammar in the Context of Writing," that the move away from systematic grammar instruction had both political and religious motivations.[62] Some people thought "that grammar should be taught as a formal system because it represents order, authority, and something that—to them—seems absolute, without question."[63] Weaver suggests that proponents of formal grammar instruction "argue for grammar on what, for them, are moral and religious grounds."[64] Weaver's point of view suggests that the rejection of formal grammar teaching is synonymous with a rejection of absolute truth or authority. Imagine if Weaver and her like-minded counterparts could remove absolute truth from the study of mathematics. What if two plus two did not always have to equal four?

> There have been two major currents in progressive education. They pertain to curricular content and pedagogical method, respectively. Both currents put progressives on a collision course with grammar. Around the turn of the century, the number of students going to high school began to increase dramatically,

> from approximately 5 percent in 1890, to 10 percent in 1900, 14 percent in 1910, and 31 percent in 1920. This historic change became the occasion of debates over the content of the curriculum. Previously, the K-12 curriculum was viewed as a narrow ladder leading to study at a college or a university and was based on the liberal arts...The great increase in the numbers of such students naturally led educators to consider revising the curriculum to make it more directly beneficial for the majority of students and geared less to the preferences of college professors.[65]

Because of the influence of this progressive view, many students, some who desire to go on to college, are graduating without the solid liberal arts foundation that they need to be successful at that level.

John Dewey is revered as the founding father of progressive education. "Central to his writings is the conviction that there was too much formalism in the schools of his day, and he was most probably right. The amount of factual information that grade school students early in the twentieth century were expected to know is incredible by contemporary standards."[66] While Dewey argued for a balance between formal and informal instruction, he never advocated for the elimination of formal instruction entirely. "In other words, there was no intrinsic opposition between the goals of progressive education and formal instruction in grammar. As long as a balance between formal and informal subjects, recommended by Dewey, was the desideratum, common sense dictated that the foundational subjects like grammar and arithmetic would continue to be taught formally."[67]

Although Dewey did not advocate for the abolition of grammar teaching, other educators took his ideas to the extreme and proposed the further minimization of liberal arts education and formal instruction.[68] One of these extremists was William Kilpatrick. "A charismatic lecturer, Kilpatrick burst on the educational scene with an influential essay in which he advocated a curriculum consisting entirely of a series of lifelike 'projects' that students would select for themselves and bring to completion in their own ways. For Kilpatrick, engagement in voluntary, purposeful activity was the only form that education should ever take. He was opposed to any subject matter that was 'fixed in advance.' Everything that a student learned was to flow naturally from volitional activity."[69] Another of these educational extremists was Franklin Bobbit who argued in 1924 that systematic training in grammar was unnecessary.[70]

Beginning in the early sixties, it became unfashionable to teach traditional grammar in American public schools. During a time when society sought peace, love, and equality, opponents of formal instruction in grammar argued against what they viewed as "a Puritanical view that equate[d] the mastery of standard written English with a person's worth and intellect."[71] As a result, they "adopted an aggressive stance, stating that empirical research prove[d] that such instruction, far from helping student writing, [was] actually harmful to it."[72] As a result, a "campaign to de-emphasize grammar"[73] began and was supported in both research and textbooks. This campaign was based largely on three studies, "The Braddock report of 1963, the Hillocks report of 1986, and the Hillocks and Smith report of 1991."[74] "Typical of the period is an influential textbook, Writing with Power, by Peter Elbow. According to Elbow, attention to grammar is not just harmful to writing; it is also dangerous to one's mental health."[75]

> Learning grammar is a formidable task that takes crucial energy away from working on your writing, and worse yet, the process of learning grammar interferes with writing; it heightens your preoccupation with mistakes as you write out each word and phrase, and makes it almost impossible to achieve that undistracted attention to your thoughts and experiences as you write that is so crucial for strong writing (and sanity). For most people, nothing helps their writing so much as learning to ignore grammar.[76]

During this time, "English teaching, both in primary schools and in secondary schools was dominated by literature and the search for creativity in writing."[77]

Many educators jumped on this bandwagon of grammar teaching prohibition because they found the task of teaching grammar to be arduous, tedious, and boring. In the book, The War Against Grammar, the author describes how teachers have shifted from direct instruction in grammar to more entertaining practices: "Apparently, their students tend to lose interest when discussion turns to conjugating verbs; so, they break out the mangoes and powdered sugar."[78] Essentially, curriculum was "dumbed down" because it was too hard and too boring. Imagine if this same ideology was applied to math. What would math curriculum and pedagogy look like today if math educators in the sixties had eliminated everything from their instruction that was too hard or too boring?

As discussed in Chapter 1, there has been a significant decline in literacy in the United States. It is important to note that during the sixties and seventies when opposition to grammar instruction became the most prevalent professional opinion, the "efficacy of language arts education in the United States declined markedly."[79] In fact, one "study by the Educational Testing Service (ETS) of adult literacy in the United States compared with the situation in other wealthy nations provides empirical indication of a problem in language arts education starting in the sixties."[80] The same report indicated that adults who entered school before the ban on grammar instruction, those fifty-six years and older, were the second most literate population while those adults entering school after the grammar ban showed mediocre performance.[81] Likewise, the decline in the nation's SAT scores, "both verbal and quantitative scores began to decline in 1963, the year of the NCTE Braddock report [which opposed formal grammar teaching]."[82] Since then, the number of remedial courses in English composition on college campuses has been on the rise. "In a 1995 survey, 78 percent of colleges and universities offered at least one remedial reading, writing, or mathematics course, and 29 percent of first-time freshmen took at least one such course."[83] Despite the fact that "the general view in education was that grammar could be safely ignored," the demise of grammar "turned out to be a dead end as it left a significant number of school leavers with hardly any reading and writing skills at all."[84]

Due to both the overwhelming data regarding the decline of literacy in the US and a resurgence of belief in the effectiveness of explicit grammar teaching, many educators are beginning to question the decision to remove grammar from English Language Arts classrooms. "Grammar scholars like Martha Kolln (1999) and Rei Noguchi (1991) and anthologies such as Susan Hunter and Ray Wallace's The Place of Grammar in Writing Instruction: Past, Present, and Future (1995) have tried to rescue grammar through advocacy scholarship and development of new approaches to teaching grammar."[85] In the last two decades, the battle over grammar teaching has continued with educators clinging to research and classroom evidence on both sides of the issue. Sadly, for many teachers, schools, and districts, "grammar remains a four-letter word."[86]

The Debate over Grammar Teaching in America

"First of all, there can be no valid objection to the study of grammar, of English or of any other language...Languages exist, they are systematic, or grammatical, and these systems and linguistic theory itself, therefore, have as much claim to be worthy of study as have solar, chemical and social systems and scientific theory."[87] In an article published in the journal College English

(1968), Ronald Wardhaugh lamented over academia's rejection of grammar teaching:

> It does seem strange that the most basic of all humanistic studies, the study of one's own language, could be so sadly and generally neglected by the very people who one would expect require it most to give them that well roundedness which they will so often claim to have. Some of us can only wonder how it is possible to discuss English literature without a rigorous training in English phonology and syntax, particularly poetic literature. Still experience tells us that it is done, in fact that such is the norm, with the sad results that what sometimes passes for profound literary insight is in actual fact profound linguistic ignorance.[88]

A Rejection of the Faulty Research against the Formal Teaching of Grammar

The research that supported the removal of grammar from lesson plans is neither valid nor reliable. "The claims that are still being made [such as it is best practice to teach grammar only in the context of student writing] suffer from innumerable problems ranging from the definition of 'teaching grammar' to the definition of 'improved writing.'"[89] There has been a renewed interest in teaching grammar partly due to the faulty research that its ban was originally based on. In the article, "On Not Teaching Grammar" (1996), Ed Vavra refutes claims made by the anti-grammar movement and argues that students cannot learn grammar simply by writing. David Mulroy is another author who criticizes educational research against grammar teaching and explains some of the problems with the research conducted by Braddock and Hillocks:

> A glance at the studies summarized by Braddock and by Hillocks clears up the mystery: All of them concern the short-term effects of instruction in formal grammar on the work of relatively mature students. For this reason, these studies have no real bearing on the value of the traditional approach to teaching grammar. From antiquity to the twentieth century, grammar was introduced to children at the beginning of their schooling, as soon as they learned how to read, and it remained a central concern for several years. It was a foundation that was built carefully and gradually in the still-receptive minds of relatively young pupils. The question to be asked then is whether a foundation of grammatical concepts laid slowly and systematically in the early grades is beneficial to students later in their academic careers. Instead of addressing that question, the research projects cited by Braddock and by

Hillocks ask what happens when you insert some grammar into the curriculum at various spots along the way. This is like trying to insert partial foundations beneath half-finished houses and concluding from ensuing debacles that foundations are useless.[90]

It is imperative that students not only learn grammar, but also that they use inquiry to study it and application to translate their learning to reading and writing.

When asked about the research that has supported removing direct grammar instruction in K-12 classrooms, Michael Clay Thompson suggested, "The people driving that research were not disciplined scholars themselves."[91] In a study entitled "Grammar for Writing: An Investigation of the Effects of Contextualized Grammar Teaching on Students' Writing," the researchers agree with Thompson. They argue that the research in the 1960s and 1970s that led to the abandonment of grammar instruction was based on the supposed "grounds that it was ineffectual in supporting language development, particularly writing development."[92] However, the research of Jones, Myhill, & Bailey (2012) indicates that "existing research is limited in that it only considers isolated grammar instruction and offers no theorization of an instructional relationship between grammar and writing."[93] The study concluded that teaching grammar in isolation must be followed by connecting it to student writing and those results must be analyzed before a claim to end all grammar instruction can be made. "Connections [must be] forged for the student writer between the grammar under focus and the learning focus for the writing."[94] It is imperative that students not only learn grammar, but also that they use inquiry to study it and application to translate their learning to reading and writing.

The Communicative Language Teaching Approach

The Communicative Language Teaching (CLT) approach "was developed in the 1970s with the belief that communicative competence consists of more than simply the knowledge of the rules of grammar."[95] This approach recommended explicit instruction in grammatical rules along with communicative application, and because of this approach, grammar rules began to reappear in textbooks.[96] "Extensive research on learning outcomes in French immersion programs...showed that, despite substantial long-term exposure to meaningful input, the learners did not achieve accuracy in certain grammatical forms. This research suggested that some type of focus on grammatical forms was necessary if learners were to develop high levels of accuracy in the target language."[97] However, what was missing was the application of learning. I would suggest that no matter what language is being studied, the grammar of that language is important knowledge for students who want to be able to read and write that language. It is recommended that teachers take an approach to grammar teaching that involves truly getting the "gist" of the English language by using inquiry into grammatical structures and choices, learning grammar as a system, and applying that knowledge to reading and writing. This approach will be explained further in Chapter 5.

The Naturalist Movement

It is recommended that teachers take an approach to grammar teaching that involves truly getting the "gist" of the English language by using inquiry into grammatical structures and choices, learning grammar as a system, and applying that knowledge to reading and writing.

"The progressive approach has been recycled continuously... and has always been presented as the latest pedagogy."[98] The Naturalist Movement is the current reincarnation of progressive education and takes a moderate approach to grammar teaching. Instead of teaching it in a systematic, traditional way, Naturalists recommended that grammar be taught in the context of student writing with no recommendation that grammar ever be taught in isolation or as a complete unit of study.

This grammar teaching only in the context of student writing approach was spurred on by the writing workshop approach where teachers circulated classrooms and conferenced with individual students about their areas of struggle. This more moderate approach "was adopted by Constance Weaver, whose book Teaching Grammar in Context is a fan favorite in National Council of Teachers of English (NCTE) circles. As her title implies, Weaver takes advantage of the loophole provided by NCTE statements against teaching grammar in isolation. As interpreted by her, however, teaching a subject in context comes very close to not teaching it at all."[99] Her approach recommends introducing only minimal grammatical terminology to students in an attempt to provide students with what she terms receptive competence. She claims, "Students need to understand what the teacher is referring to, but they do not always need enough command of the terms to use such terms themselves."[100]

The problem with the concept of receptive competence is that many state standards demand that students achieve a command of the English language. For example, the Common Core Standards state that students must "demonstrate command of the conventions of standard English grammar and usage when writing or speaking."[101] Most current state standards agree that students should be able to demonstrate command of the conventions of standard English grammar and usage when writing and speaking. In his book, The War Against Grammar (2003), David Mulroy makes a solid argument against receptive competence. He contends, "The fact that people cannot use certain terms themselves is a clear sign that they do not fully understand them."[102] Clearly, providing students with only receptive competence does not help them meet the educational standard. Mulroy continues, "Teachers who aim at 'receptive competence' are disregarding a pedagogical principle that is almost too obvious to state—viz., explanations work best when the terms employed are fully understood by all involved."[103]

Advocates for this organic method of teaching grammar in context suggest several operational principles including exposing students to many examples and texts, providing students with opportunities to use language and grammar that they have not been taught directly and have not practiced systematically, giving students opportunities to collaborate and compare writing, and encouraging revision.[104] While the Communicative Language Approach is currently popular in US education, it is based on the false assumptions that grammar can be acquired unconsciously and that the study of grammatical rules is a waste of time.[105] Models and exemplars, collaboration and comparison, and revision are all worthwhile practices, but all of those practices are even further enhanced when accompanied by direct, systematic instruction in grammar. A learner cannot show command of language if he or she cannot even name and define its parts.

The National Council of Teachers of English (NCTE)

The National Council of Teachers of English (NCTE) was founded in 1911 and now boasts over 80,000 members and thirteen journals.[106] "Over the years, NCTE publications have often provided a platform for teachers opposed to emphasizing grammar. Their anti-grammar stance is especially associated with the name of Charles Fries, a linguist from the University of Michigan."[107] Fries advocated for the application of the scientific method to language. Fries suggested that linguists should not prescribe rules for how others express themselves.

In the book The War Against Grammar, David Mulroy suggests that Fries' ideas "lent weight to the false belief that modern linguists had discredited traditional grammar."[108] Mulroy calls Fries' "harsh critique of traditional school grammar...guilty of overreaching."[109] Fries challenged the definition of a sentence as well as the definitions of the eight parts of speech since words can often serve multiple functions. However, Mulroy argues vehemently against Fries' point of view:

> In teaching the classes of words, it is natural to begin with prototypical examples. Names of persons, places, and things provide a good collection of nouns. As one continues to study grammar, more refined criteria come into play, often subconsciously…Any noun, for example, can be given an adjectival function by putting it in front of another noun. We think of chicken as being a noun, but in a phrase like chicken salad it functions as an adjective.[110]

In other words, the fact that a noun can become an adjective does not negate that it was ever a noun. Students cannot make sense of the fact that a noun can take on an adjectival function unless they first understand the definition of both a noun (a person, place, thing, or idea) and an adjective (a word that modifies a noun or pronoun).

In 1985, the NCTE adopted an official resolution that agreed with research suggesting that grammar instruction is harmful:

> Resolved, that the NCTE affirm the position that the use of isolated grammar and usage exercises not supported by theory and research is a deterrent to the improvement of students' speaking and writing and that, in order to improve both of these, class time at all levels must be devoted to opportunities for meaningful listening, speaking, reading, and writing; and that NCTE urge the discontinuance of testing practices that encourage the teaching of grammar rather than the improvement of writing.[111]

In 1991, the NCTE published Handbook of Research on Teaching the English Language Arts which contained an article called "Grammar and Usage" written by George Hillocks, Jr. and Michael Smith.[112] These authors affirmed the 1985 stance of the NCTE that "the teaching of traditional grammar is not just useless but pernicious."[113] The article argued:

> School boards, administrators, and teachers who impose the systematic study of traditional school grammar on their students over lengthy periods of time in the name of teaching writing do them a gross disservice which should not be tolerated by anyone concerned with the effective teaching of good writing.[114]

In the NCTE guidelines for teachers, the only reference to grammar suggests, "teachers should understand the significance of grammar systems as one way to discuss language, and they should understand the relationship of scholarly grammar systems to the production of language."[115] It is a curiosity that the

NCTE recognizes the value of grammar systems in producing language in their teacher guidelines but then advises against sharing that power with students.

Standards for the English Language Arts

"When the NCTE and the International Reading Association [now known as the International Literacy Association] produced 'national standards' in 1994, they neglected to include the study of correct usage as part of their subject. The consequences of this era of linguistic libertarianism...could be readily detected in the collapse of SAT verbal scores in the 1970s, the persistence of these low scores even as SAT math scores rebounded in the 1980s and 1990s, and the rise of remedial programs in reading and writing in universities, where professors became accustomed to receiving error-ridden papers from their poorly educated students."[116]

The inclusion of wording mandating that students develop a command of the conventions of language in federal and state standards acknowledges what many researchers still are not—that change is needed concerning the absence of grammar teaching in America. "The Common Core has provided a much-needed 'wakeup call' on the importance of rigorous writing, said Lucy M. Calkins, founding director of the Reading and Writing Project at Teachers College, Columbia University, a leading center for training teachers in process-oriented literacy strategies."[117] With this shift to more rigor, state standards are requiring "students to do more writing about what they've read, and less about their own lives."[118]

The Assembly for the Teaching of English Grammar (ATEG)

In recent years, some educators have begun to question the NCTE's stance on not teaching grammar. "In 1983, Ed Vavra, a literature and language arts specialist at Shenandoah College in Winchester, Virginia...began publishing a newsletter, Syntax in the Schools, dedicated to restoring interest in professional circles in grammar instruction."[119] Vavra funded the circulation of this newsletter himself and garnered enough interest and support to begin a conference. The advent of this conference "marked the birth of the Association for the Teaching of English Grammar. Three years later, the association was recognized by the NCTE as an official interest group and was renamed the Assembly for the Teaching of English Grammar, or ATEG."[120]

The ATEG has made its mission to restore "interest and respectability to the subject of grammar."[121] The ATEG takes the stance that "grammar is important because it is the language that makes it possible for us to talk about language."[122] The ATEG "advocates greater emphasis in the language arts. The group is small but gradually growing in numbers and influence. As more and more state standards prescribe the teaching of grammar, its stock is destined to rise."[123] However, many members of ATEG still hold a "negative view of traditional instruction in grammar,"[124] which limits the group's efficacy.

The History behind Grammar Schools

With all of the technology and resources at teachers' fingertips today, there is no excuse for grammar instruction to be boring.

"From the 1770s until its peak in the 1950s...grammar was so much at the center of elementary study that elementary schools became known as 'grammar schools.'"[125] "The assumption that traditional instruction in grammar was essentially misguided seems...to be the mirror image of the myth of the good old days. It is not true that English classes before the sixties were generally ineffective. Many people alive today attribute their success in large part to training received in such classes."[126] Should teachers return to boring skill and drill activities and worksheets? Of course not. Today's teachers have so many resources at the tips of their fingers. They can integrate technology and enhance their curriculum with websites such as NoRedInk. With all of the technology and resources at teachers' fingertips today, there is no excuse for grammar instruction to be boring.

THE PRESENT

CHAPTER 3

Living in the Present: Analyzing Current Trends in Grammar Teaching

Public Opinion on Grammar Teaching

The public has not always agreed with academia regarding the removal of grammar teaching from public school classrooms. "Newsweek joined the fray in 1975 by declaring that college graduates are inept writers because educators stopped teaching such basics as grammar and structure when they shifted attention to creativity. The magazine's treatise, 'Why Johnny Can't Write,' calls for writing teachers to take their classrooms back to the basics of grammar and, if necessary, go back to school themselves until they learn the fundamentals well enough to teach them. The need is urgent, Newsweek proclaims, if America is to maintain effective written communication that is vital to industry, and thus the nation as a whole."[127] A more recent source states, "The public is fed up with the academic profession's indifference to correct English."[128] After all, it seems paradoxical that English teachers would forbid the teaching of English grammar.

After all, it seems paradoxical that English teachers would forbid the teaching of English grammar.

In 1996, David Mulroy, author of The War Against Grammar (2003), attended a session on his state's academic standards and proposed that "all high school seniors should be required to identify the eight parts of speech in a selection of normal prose. He thought it a 'modest and reasonable suggestion.' To his surprise, he was plunged into controversy, supported by parents, but strongly opposed by pedagogical experts, who informed him that the NCTE disparaged the value of any grammar instruction."[129] As a result of this incident, Mulroy began to research why there is such opposition to grammar teaching. From his research, Mulroy discovered that "those who were hostile to grammar instruction cast themselves as progressives and saw proponents of instruction in grammar as rigid traditionalists."[130] Mulroy wrote his book to encourage the resurgence of grammar teaching. He says,

"Questioning the value of basic grammar is like asking whether farmers should know the names of their crops and animals."[131] Students have to understand the foundation of the English language if there is ever going to be any hope that they will be able to read it critically or write it academically.

Teacher Attitudes toward Grammar Teaching

Students have to understand the foundation of the English language if there is ever going to be any hope that they will be able to read it critically or write it academically.

"While some of today's teachers lived through an earlier era of formal and systematic training in Latin-based grammar, many younger teachers were unwitting victims of research that concluded instruction made no difference to the quality of students' writing, so why bother."[132] It has been suggested that "the problem started with teachers deciding not to teach grammar. Several decades later, many teachers could not teach grammar if they chose to because they themselves have never had any formal instruction in the subject."[133] Many teachers have insecurities about their own learning gaps in grammar, and so they avoid teaching it. Other teachers are hesitant to teach grammar because they remember language handbooks, grammar workbooks or worksheets, and sentence diagramming, which all seemed tedious and boring. Still other teachers shy away from grammar teaching because of the pressure they feel from educational leaders who are still touting anti-grammar research.

Improving teacher attitudes toward teaching grammar starts with first combatting anti-grammar research with the facts and then building teachers' self-efficacy in both content knowledge and pedagogical practices in the area of grammar.

In a personal interview with grammar guru Michael Clay Thompson, I asked him why there is such resistance among educators to teaching grammar. Thompson responded, "People never learned enough grammar themselves to feel confident teaching it."[134] One study reported, "The absence of explicit grammar teaching in the curriculum in Anglophone countries [such as the United States] for nearly 50 years has resulted in many present English teachers not having the grammatical subject knowledge (GSK) needed to teach grammar confidently."[135] This lack of knowledge leaves teachers "ill-equipped to cope with grammar teaching, but also generates anxiety, hostility, and lack of confidence toward grammar."[136] Improving teacher attitudes toward teaching grammar starts with first combatting anti-grammar research with the facts and then building teachers' self-efficacy in both content knowledge and pedagogical practices in the area of grammar.

Grammar should be recognized as an opportunity for thinking and learning, not as a punishment.

In order to change the prevailing negative attitudes toward formal grammar instruction, we have to shift how we think about it. "Grammar and mechanics no longer have to be the castor oil of writing workshop—something yucky you have to swallow before you can get to the business of writing. Grammar and mechanics are the business of shaping our writing, shaping our meaning, and creating effects that dazzle."[137] Grammar should be viewed "as a creational facility rather than a correctional one."[138] Grammar should be recognized as an opportunity for thinking and learning, not as a punishment.

Improved teacher outlooks will lead to improved student outlooks and then to improved student outcomes.

Improved teacher outlooks will lead to improved student outlooks and then to improved student outcomes. Michael Clay Thompson suggests in his book Advanced Academic Writing Volume Two that students have two possible futures when taking the challenging academic route to pursue a college or university degree. They can be filled with anxiety and uncertain about how to write an academic paper, not knowing the correct grammar and punctuation, or they can understand the foundation of the English language and proceed with confidence.[139] Why would teachers not want to ensure that students have the most confidence possible for their futures?

Many educators are beginning to realize their own lack of confidence and fear passing that on to their students.

Many educators are beginning to realize their own lack of confidence and fear passing that on to their students. They see the drastic and negative impact that removing grammar instruction has caused and are expressing renewed interest in coming up with working solutions. Teachers just need educational leadership at the federal, state, district, and building levels to come alongside them and support their effort to make some changes. It is evident that what we have been doing is not working.

The Problems with the Current Practices in Grammar Teaching

Current Practice One: Teaching Grammar Only in the Context of Student Writing

"In the US, there has been some emphasis on the notion of grammar in context (Weaver, 1996, for example), but a theoretical relationship between grammar and writing has never been adequately articulated, and the idea of 'in context' is problematic, often meaning in practice an isolated 'mini-grammar lesson' within an English lesson."[140] The concept of teaching grammar in context only is paradoxical because those who advocate for this practice suggest when teaching grammar to students in the context of writing, mini-lessons are taught in isolation. Of course, they do not use the word isolation to describe their pedagogy.

On the other hand, students who are exposed to systematic grammar instruction over time have the opportunities to make meaningful connections. These connections shape student understanding about how to use the conventions and grammatical structures of language to craft writing.

Another problem with teaching grammar only in the context of what students read and write is that while "some children will be able to induce the standard rules for themselves, ... others will not; those who cannot do this for themselves may benefit from explicit instruction."[141] What is missing in the only-in-context approach is the teaching and learning of the systematic nature of grammar. Students learn bits and pieces of the language and then struggle to apply them, but they do not understand how grammar functions together as a whole. The four levels—the parts of speech, the parts of the sentence, phrases, and clauses—build on one another to increase student understanding of the English language. For those learners who are forced to pick up grammar as they go along in the context of their own writing and are capable of doing so, even they "reach a language plateau beyond which it is very difficult to progress. To put it technically, their linguistic competence fossilizes."[142] On the other hand, students who are exposed to systematic grammar instruction over time have the opportunities to make meaningful connections. These connections shape student understanding about how to use the conventions and grammatical structures of language to craft writing.

Finally, the grammar-in-context approach is fundamentally flawed. "It treats grammar as an isolated set of rules, thereby considering the written product under review as the only relevant context for grammar instruction. It completely ignores the context from which the rules derive, the language system itself. Quite simply, students have no background knowledge about grammar, no vocabulary, no concepts, no context, no means for understanding teachers' explanations of rules or their application. Thus, someone who attempts to teach grammar in context is, in effect, attempting to teach grammar in a vacuum."[143]

Despite these problems, there are many educational leaders who are still advocating for grammar to be taught in the context of individual student writing only. Michael Thompson has argued that teaching grammar only in the context of writing "must be weighed against the probability that essential knowledge will not be taught at all."[144] Unfortunately, he is right—many teachers have taken the advice that grammar should only be taught to individual students in the context of their own writing to mean that grammar is an unessential skill that can be eliminated from lesson plans so that teachers can spend more time focusing on essential or priority standards of learning.

Current Practice Two: Teaching Grammar Only through Writing Workshop Style Individual Student Conferences

One structure through which grammar is taught in the context of student writing is known as writing workshop, a classroom practice that became popular in the 1980s. One teacher, Brenda Petruzzella, who practiced writing workshop for years, wrote an article entitled "Grammar Instruction: What Teachers Say" (1996). The article pointed out that conferencing with individual students did seem to make a positive impact on their individual writing but "was difficult to arrange in a class of 30 students, half of whom would be looking for ways to goof-off or cause disruption while [she] was on the other side of the room. And always, there was the problem of how to explain and discuss grammatical concepts with students without using grammatical terms they didn't know."[145] In my own classroom, I found that while I was conferencing with students, they could correct mistakes. Then, as soon as I walked away, they would often make the same mistakes because they did not understand the grammatical rules behind the correction. For example, I would point out a punctuation error in a compound sentence, and a student would be able to correct it with my help by choosing to use either a comma and coordinating conjunction or a semicolon. However, since the students did not have a foundational knowledge about the parts of the sentence, such as subjects and verbs, they would continue to struggle with determining sentence types, much less punctuating them correctly.

There are several problems with only teaching grammar through individual student conferences using the writing workshop model, including classroom management, time to conference with each individual student, and the

Writing workshop itself is a phenomenal class structure and is not the issue; rather, limiting grammar instruction to individual student conferences is where we fail.

inability to help students make connections between the levels of grammar. One teacher, Joan Berger, noted in her article, "A Systematic Approach to Grammar Instruction," "The more I used mini-lessons and conferencing, the more convinced I became that in addition to responding to individual problems as they arose, I also needed a plan, a systematic approach to teaching conventions of punctuation and techniques of sentence combining."[146] Berger switched her teaching pedagogy from a writing workshop approach to a systematic, direct teaching approach to grammar, which made a purposeful progression through a variety of sentence constructions. Her approach differed from traditional programs because as soon as she taught a new grammatical concept, "students [were] required to incorporate it consciously in their written pieces."[147] Berger found that after direct instruction and application, her students began to use grammatical terminology more fluently, to punctuate more correctly, and to write longer, more grammatically complex sentences.[148] Berger's conclusion was that making the requirement to apply grammar instruction to writing helps "students to transfer their new knowledge directly into their writing."[149]

In another study, a group of teacher researchers reported, "As whole-language-committed English teachers, we had for years used mini-lessons to teach grammar. Mini-lessons, however, had the unintended consequence of artificially separating language rules into discrete chunks. They were as inefficient in producing long-term student learning as were the old worksheets. Furthermore, mini-lessons had produced students who did not have a common language and knowledge base."[150] Writing workshop itself is a phenomenal class structure and is not the issue; rather, limiting grammar instruction to individual student conferences is where we fail.

Current Practice Three: Teaching Grammar Only through Sentence Combining

I would propose that while there are often exceptions to the rules, students have to first learn the rules before they can understand exceptions.

"The years following 1963 were filled with sentence-combining research that showed statistically significant results on methods that relied on practice with forms."[151] Sentence combining is a reliable method for practicing grammar, but it cannot replace direct, systematic instruction. After all, how will students be able to combine sentences correctly if they cannot identify a subject and a verb or distinguish a phrase from a clause? Sentence combining should be practiced after studying level four of grammar—clauses, but students cannot master level four if they have not first studied level one—the parts of speech, level two—the parts of the sentence, and level three—phrases. "Thorough analysis accomplishes in depth what sentence combining only touches upon, for sentence combining succeeds in drawing attention to some structures that can be used for expanding a sentence, but it provides neither method nor rationale for choosing one structure over others. Nor does it instill an understanding of the language system as a whole that gives students the control over structures they need."[152] While teaching strategies such as writing workshop, mini-lessons, conferences, and sentence combining are all worthwhile methods, they cannot take the place of direct and systematic grammar instruction. Without grammar teaching, these strategies alone do not provide students "a full grasp of the amazing intricacies of our language."[153]

Current Practice Four: Using Metaphorical Terminology Instead of Academic Vocabulary

In an attempt to make grammatical terminology easier to understand for students, some studies suggest supplementing traditional definitions of grammatical terminology with metaphors.[154] Constance Weaver advocates for teaching a limited vocabulary of grammar terms: "In-context grammar instruction should cover the least number of traditional terms necessary to teach a usage or punctuation concept."[155] Weaver "argues that the traditional definition and terms, especially the parts of speech, are not useful or entirely truthful."[156] To support her supposition, Weaver explains "that a pronoun's traditional definition is that it takes the place of a noun; however, the word 'boy' can take place of the name, 'Scott,' yet 'boy' is a noun and not a pronoun."[157] I would propose that while there are often exceptions to the rules, students have to first learn the rules before they can understand exceptions.

One major problem with teachers creating metaphorical terminology for grammatical concepts is that the terms are not standardized and do not translate from one classroom to the next. Students may have to learn even more terms than if they had learned the traditional terms due to teachers from course to course changing the terminology. In one study, students reported "that having a shared vocabulary between their English and foreign language teachers helped enormously. Students were able to unlock meaning in what they perceived as confusing eighteenth and nineteenth-century English prose once they recognized the key as being the author's use of the subjunctive—a concept that they were learning in foreign language but that had not been covered in English. Understanding direct and indirect objects helped them choose the correct pronouns in English, a concept they had already 'drilled' in Spanish class."[158] Learning English grammar would provide the same understanding if not more than learning grammar in a second language did.

A common language shared between teachers and students is important when studying any content area. "It is convenient for us to be able to refer to 'nouns,' 'verbs,' 'subjects,' and 'predicates' when talking about things like subject-verb agreement."[159] When striving to achieve competence in communicative skills such as reading, writing, speaking, and listening, a shared academic vocabulary of traditional grammar terms allows teachers and students to talk about learning goals. The ability to use these terms not only allows students to apply grammar knowledge to academic writing, but it also translates to future study of foreign languages.

Recommended Practice: An Argument for Systematic Grammar Instruction

"The overall problem with grammar instruction methods is that so far none have produced the desired result: a metacognitive application of grammar knowledge to improve one's adherence to conventions of written English."[160] Today in American public education, "approaches to grammar instruction represent a pendulum swing between passive osmosis and 'skill and drill.'"[161] However, "grammar is a demanding subject best learned at a young age when students are still forming their foundational linguistic habits. It must be taught slowly and systematically in a way that is suitable for the young. When grade school teachers understand basic concepts and teach them consistently, year after year, they endow their young students with a valuable foundation."[162] This foundation allows students to progress to the ability to write academically. Students who struggle with academic writing do so "because they don't know anything about the English language and, therefore, they cannot express themselves logically, lucidly, effectively, or productively."[163] One college composition professor, Carl Singleton, argues that he has "never had a student who understood the basics do poorly in class."[164] He suggests, "Students can be taught to write, if we put first things first and proceed in an orderly fashion."[165]

To give students the ability to write academically, we have to give them a foundational knowledge of grammar. They have to study, learn, and apply the parts of speech, the parts of the sentence, phrases, and clauses.

Author of the curriculum Grammar in a Nutshell, Diana Purser, suggests that studying grammar as a writer is comparable to studying music theory as a musician. "Music theory enables music students to see and understand the structures of music while traditional grammar concepts enable writing students to see and understand the structures of the English language."[166]

...long-term exposure to systematic grammar instruction will produce significant educational gains.

Michael Clay Thompson encourages teachers to return to traditional grammar instruction in order to ensure that students get all of the foundational knowledge they need so that they can apply their grammatical subject knowledge to their writing.[167] What educators cannot afford to do is to continue adopting a position that relegates "grammatical precision to the category of things not to do. Such an approach leaves too much to chance and erroneously interprets the high academic nature of these topics."[168]

"The bottom line has become clear: We have to find ways to teach students about grammar and mechanics at a time when they have less and less experience with the printed word."[169] To give students the ability to write academically, we have to give them a foundational knowledge of grammar. They have to study, learn, and apply the parts of speech, the parts of the sentence, phrases, and clauses. While the net educational gain of the teaching and learning of grammar might not be visible immediately or after just one semester of observation (as was noted in prior studies), long-term exposure to systematic grammar instruction will produce significant educational gains.

Standard American English and Cultural Diversity

During the last 40 years, the war against grammar teaching has been waged, in part, due to the notion that teaching standard English is oppressive.[170] One of the arguments often provided to discourage grammar teaching is that by teaching a standard language, it devalues other cultures and dialects. "Attitudes toward traditional grammar and spoken dialects have been endowed with political significance."[171] "By the early 1970s, organizations representing English teachers and English professors were insisting that students had the 'right to their own language' and that dialects deserved equal status with standard English. In one policy statement, a higher education committee of the National Council of Teachers of English (NCTE) insisted that a student's reference to 'them flowers' was just as acceptable as 'those flowers.' Of course, the policy statements and proclamations by the professors and teachers were written in flawless English, but they nonetheless declared their independence from teaching it to their students (or 'them students')."[172]

In recent news, many American citizens are calling for the eradication of systemic racism. Black Lives Matter is a movement that is advocating against police brutality and racially motivated violence. "Black Lives Matter, as a political movement and ideology, is now being woven into basic aspects of education, like the study of English."[173] In an attempt to show their solidarity with Black Lives Matter, "The English Department at Rutgers [the state university of New Jersey] announced a list of 'anti-racist' directives and initiatives for the upcoming fall and spring semesters, including an effort to deemphasize traditional grammar rules."[174] The email announcing these initiatives stated that the de-emphasis of traditional grammar and other directives are planned as a "way to contribute to the eradication of systemic inequities facing black, indigenous, and people of color."[175] Rutgers' approach will "limit emphasis on grammar/sentence-level issues so as to not put students from multilingual, non-standard 'academic' English backgrounds at a disadvantage."[176]

The premise that students who are not born into homes and families where standard English is the norm do not have an equal opportunity to education is a false narrative, and teachers should do all that is within their power to ensure that all students, regardless of their advantages and disadvantages, can learn!

Rutgers' directive to deemphasize traditional grammar has been met with both support and opposition. In a recent news interview, Carol Swain, an African American author and former professor at both Princeton and Vanderbilt Universities, was asked her opinion on this topic. The reporter asked whether the statement put out by Rutgers is "basically telling students of color they cannot grasp the language or that the language itself is somehow racist."[177] Part of Swain's response included, "Activists are really pushing for lower standards for black students...what they're saying is that black people can't learn the same way as other groups so they have to have this special treatment."[178] Citing Critical Race Theory, Swain asserts that a decision such as the one made by Rutgers' English Department will only further perpetuate racial inequality by cheating students of color out of a quality education. The same news report referenced a presidential speech given by George W. Bush on July 10, 2000, where he vowed to deal with a form of systemic racism that he termed "the soft bigotry of low expectations."[179] The president stated, "No child in America should be segregated by low expectations, imprisoned by illiteracy, [or] abandoned to frustration and the darkness of self-doubt."[180]

Proponents of standard language are often accused of having the motivation of preserving class structure.[181] "For the present, 'mistakes' occur most in the speech of the young and the dialects of the poor and of racial and ethnic minorities."[182] David Mulroy tells the story of one English as a Second Language (ESL) teacher who reported to him that "she carefully refrained from criticizing nonstandard English in the classroom and felt it was important to do so. Then she added as a humorous aside, a throw-away line, that 'of course' she policed her own daughters' grammar with fanatical vigilance."[183] This conversation raises an important question: why do teachers not want the same foundation for their students that they want for their own biological children?

"These facts have contributed to a negative stereotype. Concern with correct speech is taken as a sign that a person is…indifferent to social justice and contemptuous of cultural diversity. The stereotype is unfair: there is a strong case that the dissemination of 'good' grammar confers substantial benefits, individual and collective."[184] The premise that students who are not born into homes and families where standard English is the norm do not have an equal opportunity to education is a false narrative, and teachers should do all that is within their power to ensure that all students, regardless of their advantages and disadvantages, can learn!

Of course, there will be challenges in teaching standard English to students who are not exposed to it at home. These challenges may require teachers to alter teaching strategies and provide scaffolding to meet learners where they are. However, letting these challenges change the goals of education is a way of surrendering to the challenges themselves.[185]

It is possible to be culturally responsive by valuing both inclusivity and diversity while still teaching a standard language.

> Sentences always have and always will consist of clauses with subjects and predicates and of words that fall into classes fairly well described as verbs, nouns, adjectives, adverbs, pronouns, prepositions, conjunctions, and interjections. Individuals who understand these concepts have a distinct advantage over others where the use of language is involved—and that means everywhere. If only for the purpose of helping disadvantaged students, it should therefore be a high priority for all English teachers to find ways to deliver effective formal instruction in grammar in the middle grades of all schools, not just elite ones.[186]

It is possible to be culturally responsive by valuing both inclusivity and diversity while still teaching a standard language. Teachers "ought to recognize the injustice of allowing students to continue making basic mechanical errors that may prevent them from expressing themselves well in written assignments in [their] own or other classes or getting the job they want when they graduate."[187] In fact, "when we don't teach grammar, we stifle creativity and limit possibilities for many children. We leave them to fall back on what they intuitively know about language, and as a consequence, they simply write like they speak."[188] Students deserve to have teachers who are willing to "show them what is possible in written language and how to achieve it. All children deserve to be able to use language with intention and effect, for any purpose and in all circumstances…so if teachers don't teach what school is assessing, we are being negligent. If the only language resource kids have is what they hear in their everyday lives, then we leave behind the children who need us most."[189]

The fairest and most ethical thing that a teacher can do for any student—regardless of socioeconomic status, gender, age, race, ethnicity, or any other cultural descriptor—is to provide him or her with the foundation needed to be successful in realms where Standard American English will be required, such as college entrance exams, job interviews, and in the workplace.

It is not only possible to be both a culturally responsive teacher and to teach standard English grammar: it is necessary. The book *Becoming a Multicultural Educator: Developing Awareness, Gaining Skills, and Taking Action* states, "It is critical that teachers firmly and deeply believe that every single child can achieve at high levels and can learn. If the teacher doesn't believe this, and believe it passionately, then the students will certainly not believe it either."[190] Teachers cannot lower academic expectations because they feel sorry for students with personal challenges such as low socioeconomic status or substandard levels of support at home, and they should not change academic expectations based on ethnicity or diversity. The article "Preparing for Culturally Responsive Teaching" argues, "Teachers have to care so much about ethnically diverse students and their achievement that they accept nothing less than high-level success from them and work diligently to accomplish it."[191] Teachers must maintain high expectations for ALL students! The fairest and most ethical thing that a teacher can do for any student—regardless of socioeconomic status, gender, age, race, ethnicity, or any other cultural descriptor—is to provide him or her with the foundation needed to be successful in realms where Standard American English will be required, such as college entrance exams, job interviews, and in the workplace.

Chapter 4

Reaping the Academic Benefits of Systematic Grammar Teaching

The Link between Grammar and Metacognition

"Grammar is a method of critical thinking."[192] It allows students to build strong, consistent, and valid sentences, paragraphs, and essays. Put simply, "grammar is a way of thinking about language."[193] When students think about their own thinking, such as their own stylistic choices as writers and how they use grammatical structures to create meaning, they are engaged in the highest level of thinking known as metacognition. "Grammar is a meaning-making resource: supporting writers in making appropriate linguistic choices which help them to shape and craft text to satisfy their rhetorical intentions."[194] If teachers take this approach to grammar teaching, it is impossible for grammar to be boring. "Students enjoy things like this because…they are...involved in exploring how English works."[195] When teaching and learning grammar in the classroom, students should be engaged in inquiry, problem-solving, thinking about thinking, and application.

Declarative Knowledge versus Procedural Knowledge

"Declarative knowledge is knowledge about a particular subject area. In reference to grammar studies, declarative knowledge indicates a student's ability to memorize grammar rules."[196] Procedural knowledge, on the other hand, "is the ability to do something specific. In reference to grammar studies, procedural knowledge indicates the ability to correctly use grammar in everyday life."[197] As students move from declarative knowledge to procedural knowledge, they move from memorization to application. They take what they have learned through direct, systematic instruction and through four-level sentence analysis and apply it in their own academic writing. Teachers must help students shift to a higher level of thinking by acquiring procedural knowledge instead of just declarative knowledge. It is not enough for a student to be able to state the difference between a compound sentence and a complex sentence; the student must be able to use both sentence types in writing and to make choices as a writer about which sentence type is more useful in each case. For example, if the student has two equally important things to say, he or she should choose a compound sentence where both independent clauses are equal in value. If the student has two things to say with one being less important, he or she should choose a complex sentence where the subordinate, or dependent, clause is the less important part of the sentence. By learning to make choices such as this as writers, students learn communicative competence.

Growth through Struggle

Like arithmetic, grammar can be both elementary yet, at times, difficult. It requires thought. "The inclusion of a difficult subject in a curriculum at any point is bound to have an adverse short-term effect on student performances in related subjects because students have finite amounts of time and energy. If we make students jog for a mile every morning, we will find that they have less energy on the playground at lunch, but this does not mean that jogging is bad for their long-term physical conditioning."[198] Likewise, the inclusion of grammar—taught systematically and regularly—has the potential to have significant and positive long-term effects on student performance.

Giving Students the Ability to both Follow and Break Prescriptive Rules

Language is a living, breathing organism that evolves over time. The rules and nuances of language are constantly changing. "Usages that are considered incorrect today will be perfectly proper tomorrow."[199] However, students are capable of both learning the rules that are agreed upon in Standard American English and understanding that the rules will continue to change. These two ideas—the prescriptive rules of grammar and the shifting nature of language—can peacefully coexist. "Grammar, after all, is a description of the regularities in a language, and knowledge of these regularities provides the learner with the means to generate a potentially enormous number of original sentences... The teaching of grammar offers the learner the means for potentially limitless linguistic creativity."[200] Students must be able to identify and practice the regularities of language so that they can later recognize the irregularities.

The Link between Grammar and the Study of Language

Grammar teaching is an essential part of language teaching. "Grammatical competence is one of communicative competence. Communicative competence involves knowing how to use the grammar and vocabulary of the language to achieve communicative goals, and knowing how to do this in a socially appropriate way. Communicative goals are the goals of learners studying [the] English language. So grammar teaching is necessary to achieve the goals."[201] An inability to understand grammatical rules translates into an inability to both write complete, coherent sentences and to speak English fluently and accurately.

Foreign Language Study

Students need a foundation in grammar in their first language in order to be more successful at studying a second language. "Grammar is crucial to the study of foreign language. By mastering English grammar, [students] will dramatically increase [their] ability to master foreign languages, at a time when foreign language study is more important than ever."[202] Grammar is important because it supports foreign language learning. "Explicit instruction is an important part of grammar-teaching and is easier if the pupils already have some understanding of how their first language works."[203] For example, if English-speaking students already have a foundational knowledge about verbs and verb tenses, learning how Spanish verbs change endings based on tense comes much easier.

Second Language Acquisition

Grammar not only benefits English speakers learning a second language, but it also benefits speakers of other languages who are working to acquire English as a second language. "Recent research has demonstrated the need for formal instruction for learners to attain high levels of accuracy. This has led to a resurgence of grammar teaching, and its role in second language acquisition has become the focus of much current investigation."[204] As we have established, accuracy does not just happen naturally for students whether they are studying their first language or their second. It is unfair to suggest that students who find themselves in an English-speaking country without mastery of that language should just "sit around and read novels until [their] brain[s] kick in and fluent, accurate writing starts to flow from [their] pens."[205]

In a panel discussion on "Teaching Grammar in Today's Classroom" held in 2008, Betty Azar, a university professor, weighed in on the success of ESOL students in her freshman English classes:

I consistently observed that second language students in my freshman English writing classes who had a good grounding in basic grammar (nothing fancy, but at least the ability to find a subject and a verb) were much more likely to have the language skills expected at the university level, to have the kind of interlanguage that would at least give them the opportunity to compete successfully at an American university and hopefully reach their academic and career goals...I believed then and I believe now that those who advocated zero grammar were simply wrong.[206]

"According to Azar (2007), the role of grammar is to 'help students discover the nature of language, i.e., that language consists of predictable patterns that make what we say, read, hear, and write intelligible.'"[207] The teacher's role is to lead students to discovery of grammatical patterns in order to improve students' proficiencies in speaking, reading, listening, and writing.

Shakespearean Syntax

"Grammar shows us the beauty and power of our own minds. With only eight kinds of words and two sides (subject and predicate) of each idea, we can make the plays of Shakespeare, or the novels of Toni Morrison, or the poems of Elizabeth Bishop. No system, so elegant, could be expected to make such language."[208] Not only does understanding grammatical structures help students become better academic writers, but it also helps them make sense of complex texts such as the works of Shakespeare. Shakespeare is difficult to read because he inverted traditional syntax. Shakespeare often made up word spellings, left out letters in words, and even changed the order of the words in the sentences to fit the rhythm of his writing. If students know what is standard in English grammar and syntax, such as the pattern of subject, followed by action verb, followed by object, then they can rearrange his sentences to make sense of them. Students who understand the traditional subject-verb pattern can also invert it, realizing that if Shakespeare wrote, "I, the sandwich ate," he may have meant, "I ate the sandwich."

The Link between Grammar and Academic Writing

"Grammar and writing are so inextricably linked as to be virtually synonymous. To study one is to study the other."[209] "The first step in mastering any field is gaining an overview of its structure, which requires classification of its elements."[210] "Grammatical terms are part of an orderly set of concepts that describe the organizational features of all intelligible speech and writing."[211] Students must have a grammatical understanding of the parts of speech, the parts of the sentence, phrases and clauses, and how those concepts work in order to be able to use language to construct academic writing.

The goal of grammar teaching is not just for students to memorize a lot of grammatical terms—although that will happen naturally. "The goal of grammar teaching is to help students create an interlanguage that is increasingly fluent and accurate in the use of English structures in meaningful communication."[212] In order to be successful at the type of academic writing required at the university level, students have to learn to write in a grammatically correct way. One educator reported in the English Journal (2003) that as she "explored the reasons behind students' difficulties with organization, coherence, and revision, and as [she] developed strategies for addressing the root causes, [she] found [she] was teaching grammar—not usage—but grammar, the relationship between structure and meaning."[213]

Creative Writing versus Academic Writing

"Writing is a form of communication and communication is a form of transportation. Written communication, for example, transports ideas from the writer's brain to the readers'."[214] Creative writing focuses on voice and word choice, while academic writing focuses on content, ideas, and organization. In a personal interview, Michael Clay Thompson pointed out that while creative writing is colloquial and low level concerning academic rigor, it does have its place in the classroom when building confidence in students. However, it cannot be the predominant form of writing when preparing students for the university.[215] Common types of academic writing can include expository writing (writing to explain, describe, provide information, or communicate knowledge), persuasive writing (writing making the case for or against an issue), and inquiry writing (writing to ask a question, gather data, and answer the question).[216] Types of academic writing that are often required on high-stakes standardized test writing prompts include argumentative writing (writing to argue for a claim and against a counterclaim) and text-dependent literary analysis (writing that requires thorough analysis of and citation from one or more texts).

"Teachers who argue against teaching grammar are, in fact, limiting the writing of many students to recreational use only. How often do English teachers say, 'They write fine when we're doing narratives, but when we get to expository writing, everything falls apart'? 'Everything' usually includes grammar."[217] In order to be able to perform academic writing, students must have a foundation of knowledge about what academic writing looks like; they need grammar instruction. Of course, teachers want students to write creatively with voice and passion, but they must also "write using the standard conventions of English usage and grammar that make the writing meaningful."[218]

Requirements for Well-Crafted Academic Writing

"Academic writing depends upon a prior knowledge of grammar concepts and standards."[219] The book Academic Writing (2016) by Andrew P. Johnson outlines eleven fundamentals for academic writing such as sticking to the facts, avoiding irrelevant details, and excluding useless adjectives. In addition to these tips, Johnson's book includes an entire chapter outlining nine grammatical errors that should be avoided in academic writing. His advice includes:

- Stay consistent with tense.
- Stay consistent with plurality.
- Double pronouns and noun-pronoun combinations should make sense when one is missing.
- Use that for essential clauses and which for nonessential clauses.
- Use that and which for nonhuman entities and who or whom to indicate humans.
- Use who if you can substitute he or she in the sentence; use whom if you can substitute him or her in the sentence.
- Do not end a sentence with a preposition.
- Do not use run-on sentences.
- A comparison must compare something to something else.[220]

Similarly, in his book *Advanced Academic Writing Volume 2*, Michael Clay Thompson explains several common grammar problems that must be avoided in academic writing. These errors include subject/verb disagreement, sentence fragments, run-on sentences, comma splices, pronoun case and reference errors, dangling and misplaced modifiers, split infinitives, faulty parallelism, and double negatives.[221] Whatever list of grammar errors to avoid that you want to work from, the solution is to provide students with a working knowledge of grammatical systems, including the parts of speech, the parts of the sentence, phrases, and clauses.

Punctuation as a Function of Grammar

"Punctuation is the art of marking grammar so that written ideas are not confusing."[222] It is impossible to use punctuation correctly without understanding the grammatical structures, such as phrases and clauses, which are being punctuated.[223] This is true because "punctuation rules are grammar intensive."[224] For example, a writer cannot punctuate an introductory participial phrase correctly with a comma if the writer does not even know that the introductory participial phrase exists. According to Michael Clay Thompson, "you cannot guess your way through academic punctuation."[225] In the book *Mechanically Inclined: Building Grammar, Usage, and Style into Writer's Workshop*, Jeff Anderson states, "Knowledge of conventional nuances makes the difference between 'Let's eat Grandma' and 'Let's eat, Grandma.' Or, 'I'm SO thirsty!!!' and 'I'm…sooooo…thirsty…'"[226]

Figure 4.1. Cartoon Showing the Importance of Punctuation

In the book *Eats, Shoots, & Leaves: The Zero Tolerance Approach to Punctuation*, Lynne Truss writes, "Proper punctuation is both the sign and the cause of clear thinking."[227]

Figure 4.2. Cartoon Showing the Importance of the Comma

Moving Beyond Error Correction

Understanding grammar is not just about error correction. In fact, "language is the core of all content. If you are strong in language, that gives you strength in every subject you study."[228] The ATEG suggests, "Teaching grammar will not make writing errors go away. Students make errors in the process of learning, and as they learn about writing, they often make new errors, not necessarily fewer ones. But knowing basic grammatical terminology does provide students with a tool for thinking about and discussing sentences. And lots of discussion of language, along with lots of reading and lots of writing, are the three ingredients for helping students write in accordance with the conventions of standard English."[229]

While students will correct some errors and make new ones as they learn, the important part about error correction is that understanding grammar gives them the power to be able to think about correctness.

Conventions...guide us through text. They offer clues about meaning, challenge our imaginations, provoke images, conjure up characters in our heads, and affect what we think and feel as we read. Creative and skillful use of conventions allows students' voices to be heard. It gives them power... That power shows up everywhere: in e-mail, on a resume, on a job or college application letter or essay, in a poem to a friend or sweetheart, in a letter to the editor, in a first published work—and yes, in any on-demand writing situation.[230]

Improving All Writing Domains through the Study of Grammar

One reason that critics of grammar teaching often use to discourage it is that conventions are typically only a small part of any writing rubric required by teachers or even standardized tests. However, using grammar correctly improves writing in multiple areas. Yes, conventions such as spelling, grammar, punctuation, and capitalization will improve with a better grammatical knowledge. However, other domains of writing, such as voice, word choice, sentence fluency, and organization, will improve as well. Here are just a few examples of the impact of grammar knowledge on other domains:

If students use their knowledge of clauses (level four of grammar study) to write more complex sentence structures rather than all simple sentences, it will improve both the sentence fluency and the organization of their writing. Writing will sound less repetitive and elementary. Writing will flow better from idea to idea and paragraph to paragraph.

If students are able to use their knowledge of the parts of speech (level one of grammar study) to choose more vivid verbs and precise nouns, it will improve both the voice and word choice of their writing.

If students are able to use their knowledge of phrases (level three of grammar study) to rename people or things with appositives, it will improve the voice of the writing. For example, instead of writing, "Mrs. Smith gave me an A on the assignment. Mrs. Smith is my math teacher," a student has the tools to avoid redundancy. Now, the student can write, "Mrs. Smith, my math teacher, gave me an A on the assignment."

THE FUTURE

Chapter 5

Looking Ahead: The Future of Grammar Teaching in America

What We Can Learn from Advancements in England

Encouraging developments in the reinstitution of grammar teaching are taking place in England. In fact, "the best hope for massive empirical evidence in favor of teaching grammar in the early grades lies in England's current reform."[231] Like America, England also shifted away from traditional grammar teaching in the sixties.[232] "British schools, like ours, went through a long sojourn into grammatical illiteracy. Until 1960, Truss writes [in the book Eats, Shoots & Leaves] every British school routinely taught punctuation. Then, for more than a quarter of a century, during the 'dark-side-of-the-moon years in British education…teachers upheld the view that grammar and spelling got in the way of self-expression."[233]

However, England reversed its stance on teaching grammar in 1980 and experienced "a 'rebirth of grammar teaching.'"[234] In 1998, "Britain's New Labour government made grammatical analysis the central point of its National Literacy Strategy, an integrated syllabus for teaching reading and writing in England's primary schools."[235] In 1999, "inspectors from the Office of Standards in Education concluded that teachers' poor knowledge of grammar and punctuation had contributed to problems in teaching writing. In response, Education Secretary David Blunkett, who is spearheading the campaign to revive grammar, distributed a 216-page guide on teaching grammar to all primary schools and provided funding for all fifth- and sixth-grade teachers to attend one day of training on the new material."[236] "The Queen's English Society, whose remit is the preservation of the English language, maintains that grammar is important for the 'diagnosing of faults or problems in one's own writing and in that of others.'"[237] As a result, students in England are being expected to study their own language, and test scores are on the rise once again.

The Curriculum Standards Movement

Although teaching grammar in American public school classrooms has been taboo for a number of years, things are beginning to change. "In recent years, parents and politicians have attempted to mandate more attention to [grammar] among other subjects through new academic standards."[238] Michael Clay Thompson said in a personal interview that the Common Core State Standards initiative was a good first step, but still more work needs to be done in order to implement a lucid and valid model of systematic grammar instruction.[239]

Recommendations for Future Pedagogy and Practice

Teacher Preparation

The majority of practicing teachers do not believe that they were well prepared to teach grammar. "Most teachers don't know enough about how the English language works [aka grammar], and this inevitably impacts upon student literacy outcomes."[240] The problem is that "colleges have not prepared most English teachers to teach [grammar]. Finding comma splices is one thing. But what about inviting students to analyze the structure of any sentence they read or write? Most English teachers can't do this themselves."[241] Teacher preparation programs have to address the fact that teachers are graduating with degrees certifying them to teach English without ever having studied the structure of that very language. Colleges and universities should make an English Grammar class a mandatory part of any course of study leading to teacher licensure. I found that in my home state of South Carolina, one grammar class is required to earn certification as a secondary English teacher; however, this is not a requirement for elementary and middle school teachers of English. While a grammar class is required to teach high school English, the courses for most university teacher preparatory programs are listed as either Linguistics or Modern Grammar and focus more on the development of language or the impact of structural grammar rather than the systematic grammar K-12 students need to be taught. In fact, when working to add on Secondary Certification to my teaching certificate, I had a Bachelor's degree in English and a Master's degree in Teaching and still found myself short one grammar class. I searched all of the surrounding universities for such a class and ended up having to complete an independent

Learning English grammar can no longer be a recommendation in teacher preparation programs; it must be a requirement if English teachers are going to be experts in their content.

study with a professor since no one else had signed up to take the one grammar class I could find. More recently, one state university has begun to offer a survey of grammar class, but it is recommended, not required, for English teachers. Learning English grammar can no longer be a recommendation in teacher preparation programs; it must be a requirement if English teachers are going to be experts in their content.

Teacher Attitudes toward the Teaching of Grammar

Better teacher training will help to improve teacher attitudes toward teaching grammar which will also increase the effect of teaching grammar. "Effects of teaching grammar are influenced by teachers' own attitudes towards and knowledge of language, as well as the instructional methods they use."[242] Teachers have to be experts at the structure of the English language in order to be able to appreciate it themselves and to foster that appreciation within others. Teachers "need to be [able] to understand how effective writing works, so they can notice language and teach it to their students."[243] For example, we "know that when [writers] start their sentence with words about where (adverbial phrases) rather than who, that their reader will be pulled into the setting rather than focused immediately on the character. [Writers] know that describing a character through their actions (adverbials) can sometimes be more evocative than describing their appearance (adjectivals)."[244] It is through these subtle nuances of language and stylistic choices that writers express themselves, and only readers who understand the structure of the language that they are written in will pick up on all of them.

Vertical Planning for Kindergarten through Grade 12

One of the very first things that must be done to implement systematic grammar teaching is that teachers and departments of education must adjust the curriculum. The ineffectiveness of formal grammar teaching in the past has been due in part to not teaching it in the correct order as a system. Therefore, I recommend that students be exposed to systematic grammar teaching each year so that they can master the four levels over time. See Appendix C for a Vertical Planning Pacing Guide for English Language Standards. This pacing guide is based on the recognition "that writing proficiency develops over a period of twelve years or more."[245] Students begin in elementary school learning a few parts of speech, what a complete sentence looks like, and basic end punctuation. The pacing guide provides "a sequenced approach to grammar instruction that is designed to build students' competence gradually."[246] Each year, the curriculum compounds until English 4 or the 12th grade when students have been exposed to all four levels of grammar in their entirety.

Systematic Instruction in the Four Levels of Grammar

The Assembly for the Teaching of English Grammar (ATEG) issued a position statement called "On the Value of Systematic Grammar Study." This statement recognizes that current NCTE standards mandate "significant attention to the nature of structure of language."[247] The statement also admits that despite the guidelines approved by NCTE called Content Knowledge for Effective ELA Teachers, there is a deficiency in teacher content knowledge in the area of language. Finally, the statement admits that pedagogies exist that "acknowledge grammar as a dynamic, evolving system that is responsive to local culture, acquired over a lifetime in varying contexts, and highly functional within those contexts."[248] The resolution published by the ATEG states: "Therefore, be it resolved that The Assembly for the Teaching of English Grammar (ATEG) recognize the value of systematic grammar study for teachers and students through pedagogies that promote not only the conscious knowledge of language structure but also an awareness of how language works."[249]

So what is the system that teachers should teach? Perhaps the best person to answer that question is Michael Clay Thompson. "During a period of thirty years, Michael Clay Thompson was a classroom teacher, middle school head, and academic. Now Michael is an author [of more than 100 books] and a consultant...An acclaimed speaker and workshop presenter, through his teaching, books, and presentations, he has inspired thousands of students and educators with a new love of language and literature."[250] In addition to these accolades, Thompson was "formerly a consultant to the Center for Gifted Education at the College of William and Mary, consultant and Lead Scholar for the National Javits Project for Language Arts, and President of the Indiana Gifted Association."[251]

In his book, *Grammar Voyage*, Thompson[252] suggests that there are four levels of grammar that build upon one another: the parts of speech (level one), the parts of the sentence (level two), phrases (level three), and clauses (level four). It is important that students learn grammar in this order because it forms a complex system. For example, prepositional phrases can be either adverbial because they modify a verb, adjective, or adverb in the sentence or adjectival because they modify a noun in the sentence. Therefore, a student cannot identify and use prepositional phrases correctly (level three) without first understanding the definitions of a preposition, an adjective, and an adverb (level one). Yet, many teachers skip right to teaching prepositional phrases without making sure students have the required foundational knowledge of level one. Likewise, a gerund phrase (level three) functions as a noun (level one) in the sentence. It can do anything that a noun can do; it can be the

subject, indirect object, direct object, subject complement that is predicate nominative, or object of the prepositional phrase (level two). Students will not truly grasp gerund phrases (level three) without first understanding the definition of a noun (level one) and how a noun functions in a sentence (level two). See Appendix A for a detailed list of the four levels of grammar.

When students are provided with a solid foundational understanding of the structure of the English language (i.e. grammar), they produce better academic writing. One article in support of teaching grammar expands on this idea: "Understanding the structure and relationships [of Standard American English] contributes to an increased awareness of options in writing, of opportunities for combining, embedding, controlling emphasis, and enhancing clarity."[253] As students learn how the four levels of grammar connect, "grammar and writing finally meld, where expanding and developing structure fuses with finding and creating meaning."[254]

Creating Meaning beyond Error Correction through Application in Writing

Students will produce more grammatically correct academic writing if English teachers will model their pedagogy after the following steps:

1. **Inquire**—Allow students to practice inquiry by noticing what they see authors doing in well-written texts.
2. **Learn**—Teach the four levels of grammar (the parts of speech, the parts of the sentence, phrases, and clauses) in order. Then, provide many opportunities for students to practice thinking about language as a complex system through in-depth four-level sentence analysis.
3. **Apply**—Guide students in applying their knowledge of grammatical structures to their own writing.

Application is an important part of systematic grammar teaching that is often overlooked. "Grammar and grammatical terms should be used as a tool to teach students how sentences work, including such things as how the human brain might process sentences and how different constructions do different things for different groups of writers"[255]. After teaching students the four levels of grammar and allowing students to think through four-level analyses, teachers must "help students to identify—in their own writing—the various grammatical constructions"[256]. One article from *Voices in the Middle* recommends that teachers have students complete "brief writings to practice using a particular grammatical construction…as a prelude to writing another piece where [they] simply encourage students to experiment with the options they've been learning"[257]. For example, after direct instruction and

modeling on the topic of simple and compound sentences, students could practice distinguishing between the two in a model student essay, complete a practice activity on sentence types on www.noredink.com, or engage in a team competition locating various sentence types in the newspaper. However, the final phase of application is most important. Students must take what they have learned and apply it to their own writing. A teacher could assign a one-page paper that must have no more than fifty percent of the sentences written with simple sentence structures. Students could also go back to a piece of writing that they previously produced to tally their sentence structures and set goals for growth in this area.

In the article, "How to Teach Grammar, Analytical Thinking, and Writing: A Method that Works," Lynn Sams explains why both traditional grammar instruction and the in-context approach that is popular today have both failed:

I realized why twentieth-century researchers concluded that direct instruction in grammar had no impact upon writing. Quite simply, the grammar instruction in these studies was not related to writing. It merely taught prescription (usage and rules) and description (noun, verb, prepositional phrase), the naming of parts. I realized also why the 'in-context' approach to grammar instruction advocated today has negligible impact upon writing. It consists of little more than guided application of rules that teachers seem to mysteriously pull out of a hat in order to correct errors they detect in a piece of writing. Both traditional and in-context approaches to grammar instruction fail for exactly the same reason: they treat grammar as something that exists apart from and outside of the writing process itself.[258]

Best practice in grammar instruction should include a cycle between inquiry into what good writers do, direct and explicit instruction in the four levels of grammar, practice of those skills along with four-level analysis of sentence structures, and application of those skills to writing. "As students practice the pattern, they learn the terminology. As [students and teachers] use the terminology, they practice the pattern."[259] Formal instruction and isolated skill-and-drill exercises "with no connection to what students are reading or writing result in just that—isolated skills with no connection to what students are reading or writing. But systematic grammar and usage instruction connected to what students are reading and writing [is] valuable."[260] "Students become better editors of their own writing and stronger critics of others' writing when they are exposed to a steady diet of sentence possibilities, explicit instruction in the punctuation of those sentence patterns, and orchestrated practice of those patterns. This type of systematic instruction that is tied to their own writing helps students write better."[261]

Student objectives and essential questions for grammar standards should be written in such a way that they demonstrate both mastery of the learning and application to communicative skills. In the article, "Bridging the Grammar Gap: An Interdisciplinary Approach," the teacher researchers give an example of a possible objective statement when teaching the grammatical concept of subjunctive verb mood: "Students will understand and apply the concepts of active/passive voice and the subjunctive mood to critical reading and thoughtful writing."[262] Application after understanding is the key.

The Importance of Practice

"While not denying a role for explicit instruction, N. Ellis (2002) suggests that language learning is ultimately implicit in nature, 'the slow acquisition of form-function mappings and the regularities therein. This skill, like others, takes tens of thousands of hours of practice, practice that cannot be substituted for by provision of a few declarative rules.'"[263] In order for grammar teaching to be effective, there must be a combination of direct teaching, practice of skills, and application to writing. "Current research indicates that learners need opportunities to both encounter and produce structures which have been introduced either explicitly, through a grammar lesson, or implicitly, through frequent exposure."[264]

Four-Level Sentence Analysis Instead of Diagramming Sentences

Many critics of sentence diagramming argue that this practice does little more than teach students how to diagram sentences—there is no translation to writing. To these arguments, Lynn Sams responds, "this can be true if one chooses to teach it that way."[265] However, Sams believes that the process of diagramming sentences "consists of analyzing sentences through a process of questioning that reveals the precise relationship of every part to the whole. And in order to ensure that every student works through the mental steps of the analysis, [she has] them record their steps on paper in a useful graphic organizer known as the sentence diagram."[266] Sams contends that teachers should "approach sentence analysis as a process of questioning. Because language is a system of relationship, in any given sentence every word answers a question about another word, and every structure (group of words) answers a question about another word or structure."[267]

A more modern approach to sentence diagramming is four-level sentence analysis. Four-level analysis is a method of teaching grammar systematically in the four levels: the parts of speech, the parts of the sentence, phrases, and clauses. Students write down a sentence and then analyze it by labeling each of the four levels in order and on a separate line. Students are able to use level one to figure out the answers for level two, the answers for levels one and two to figure out the answers to level three, and so on. Below is an example of a four-level sentence analysis.

Like	a	little	child,	my	father	loved	opening	presents.
prep.	adj.	adj.	n.	adj.	n.	v.	n.	n.
					subj.	AVP	------------D.O.------------	
----------prep. phrase---------							-------gerund phrase------	
--independent clause---------------------------------- a simple declarative sentence								

Here we see a gerund phrase used as the direct object. Gerund phrases are nouns, so we always see them in the normal noun places. The noun *presents* is the object of the gerund *opening*.

Figure 5.1. Example of a Four-Level Sentence Analysis

Traditional grammarians in support of grammar teaching accept "the behavioral concept of learning that equates practice with habit formation."[268] Michael Clay Thompson agrees with the premise that practice helps form healthy habits. "What I have seen in a consistent process during a period of decades is that by continuing to do four-level analysis, my thinking about language keeps getting clearer, and clearer, and clearer...You keep doing four-level analysis in your pursuit of language just as a pianist keeps practicing piano in the pursuit of music. Both music and language are vast, bottomless, hopelessly beyond our abilities to understand them completely...They cannot be finally mastered."[269]

Four-level sentence analysis leads students to inquiry. They are required to think about language. "Four-level analysis is in part a logic of sentence construction. With each example you see more clearly how and why to make a verb agree with its subject, how to structure a good introductory participial phrase, how to punctuate a complex sentence, how to edit out junky modifiers, how to do the ten thousand things that writers want to do."[270] This type of sentence analysis is not just a worksheet or a bell-ringer activity that students will complete and then discard. "What students can acquire [through four-level analysis] is a four-level mind, an ongoing and exciting awareness of how words and sentence structure and phrases and clauses operate in their language environment, which includes everything they hear and read and write."[271] For these reasons, "four-level grammar must precede the instruction of academic writing."[272] It is the vehicle in which students learn what well-constructed sentences look like so that they can later apply this knowledge in their own writing. Before students can write great paragraphs, they have to be able to write great sentences. Before students can write great sentences, they have to be able to identify them.

GIST Teaching Strategy

I created the Grammar Inquiry and System Teaching (GIST) Strategy as a visual aid to remind educators how to move beyond engaging students in rote memorization of grammatical rules by truly helping them get the "gist" of the English language. Teaching students to memorize grammatical terms alone will not help students overcome problems with analyzing sentence structures and applying them in their writing.[273] Instead, grammar must be discovered through inquiry, taught and practiced as a complex system, and applied to reading and writing. It is imperative that teachers use this teaching strategy because "when teachers do more than 'cover' grammar, writers will improve their writing by using the grammar they have learned."[274] There are three levels of thinking and learning involved in the GIST Strategy—inquiry into grammatical structures and choices, learning grammar as a complex system, and application of grammar to reading and writing. Students should inquire, learn, and apply daily!

GIST

Grammar Inquiry and System Teaching

Grammar must be discovered through inquiry, taught as a complex system, and applied to reading and writing!

INQUIRE	LEARN	APPLY
Inquiry into Grammatical Structures and Choices	Learning Grammar as a Complex System	Application of Grammar to Reading and Writing
Students acquire implicit knowledge of grammatical constructions by thinking about language. Students analyze authors' choices in style, usage, and syntax. Students evaluate their own choices as writers.	Students build their explicit knowledge of syntax by learning the four levels of grammar that build on each other and form a complex system—the parts of speech, the parts of the sentence, phrases, and clauses. They practice four-level sentence analysis and sentence combining.	Students apply their learning to their reading, writing, and speaking. They form more complex sentence structures in their writing. They use punctuation as a function of grammar. They use the levels of grammar to identify the main idea of each sentence that they read and write.

The Parts of Speech . The Parts of the Sentence . Phrases . Clauses

Figure 5.2. The GIST Strategy

Inquiry into Grammatical Structures and Choices

Inquiry into grammatical structures and choices involves students acquiring implicit knowledge of grammatical constructions by thinking about language. Students can build this knowledge by analyzing authors' choices in style, usage, and syntax and by evaluating their own choices as writers. "The best way to teach grammar is through exemplary literature. This is where grammar is real. This is where we understand the ways in which we can play with language to achieve our intentions. In great writing we can notice how the author uses their language knowledge and how they organize their words and sentences to make us notice, feel, see, or imagine something."[275]

Learning Grammar as a Complex System

Learning grammar as a complex system involves students building their explicit knowledge of syntax by learning the four levels of grammar—the parts of speech, the parts of the sentence, phrases, and clauses—and how those levels build on each other and work together to form a complex system. Each year as students study the four levels, they delve deeper into each level so that mastery of the content is achieved by the end of high school. After direct instruction, students should practice skills like four-level sentence analysis and sentence combining.

Application of Grammar to Reading and Writing

The application of grammar to reading and writing is a crucial part of this strategy because it allows students to apply their learning to their own reading, writing, and speaking. Students can form more complex sentence structures in their writing. They can use punctuation correctly because they understand that it is a function of grammar. They can use the four levels of grammar to identify the main idea of each sentence that they read and write. Application is imperative because it allows teachers to "help students to identify—in their own writing—the various grammatical constructions about which we talk."[276]

The application of grammar knowledge to reading and writing also increases student engagement. "Students find grammar most interesting when they apply it to authentic texts. Try using texts of different kinds, such as newspapers and the students' own writing, as sources for grammar examples and exercises. This approach helps make grammar relevant and alive."[277]

Teaching Grammar in Units

My final suggestion is to teach four grammar units throughout the year, one on each level of grammar—the parts of speech, the parts of the sentence, phrases, and clauses. These four units should span no more than six weeks of total instructional time in the middle school grades. Teaching these units can be accomplished simultaneously all in the first nine weeks or spaced out throughout the first three nine weeks. The students who participated in this study learned the parts of speech (two-week unit) and the parts of the sentence (one-week unit) during the first nine weeks along with a narrative writing unit. They learned phrases (two-week unit) during the second nine weeks along with units on writing objective summaries and argumentative essays. Finally, they studied clauses (one-week unit) during the third nine weeks, followed by writing units during the third and fourth nine weeks on text-dependent analysis and literary analysis essays. All four grammar units were completed in time for students to spend one and a half grading periods practicing their cumulative grammar knowledge by applying it to academic writing before state testing. In a perfect world where grammar was taught year to year in kindergarten through 12th grade, I would choose to frontload the year by completing all grammar instruction in the first nine weeks. However, I found that since my students did not usually have a solid foundation from prior years, they were less overwhelmed by breaking it up into the first three quarters. See Figure 5.3 for an excerpt taken from my syllabus for English I showing the instructional units covered during the school year.

1st Nine Weeks	2nd Nine Weeks	3rd Nine Weeks	4th Nine Weeks
Reading			
Night by Elie Wiesel Short Story Unit	*Cast Two Shadows* by Ann Rinaldi *The Odyssey* by Homer translated by Robert Fitzgerald	*Romeo and Juliet* by William Shakespeare Poetry	Choice of Classic Novel for Literature Circles *The Diary of Anne Frank* by Frances Goodrich and Albert Hackett
Writing			
Constructed Responses Personal Narratives and Memoirs Short Stories MLA Research Paper	Objective Summaries Argumentative Essays and Speeches	Text-Dependent Essays Poetry	Literary Analyses Text-Dependent Essays
Word Study			
SAT Vocabulary Grammar Word Stems Academic Vocabulary	SAT Vocabulary Academic Vocabulary	SAT Vocabulary Academic Vocabulary Shakespearean Syntax	Context Clues Practice Standardized Testing High-Frequency Words
Grammar			
Parts of Speech Active and Passive Verbs Verb Moods Parts of a Sentence Subject/Verb Agreement Pronoun/ Antecedent Agreement Parallel Structure	Phrases: Noun, Verbal, Adjectival, Adverbial, Prepositional, and Absolute	Clauses: Sentence Structures and Purposes; Noun Clauses, Relative Clauses, and Adverbial Clauses	Punctuation Study Practice EOC Questions
Speaking & Listening			
Short Story Socratic Seminars	Cast Two Shadows Project Presentations	Poetry Slam	Literature Circles

Figure 5.3. Overview of Instructional Units from Dr. Roach's Syllabus for English I

It is also important to note that while I encourage teaching grammar units in isolation, I also encourage application of each grammar topic to either reading or writing daily in the classroom. An example of the agenda portion of my lesson plan for one class period is below.

Unit: Grammar Level One—The Parts of Speech

Lesson: Coordinate and Cumulative Adjectives

Standard: 5.2a Demonstrate command of the conventions of standard English capitalization, punctuation, and spelling when writing. Use a comma to separate coordinate adjectives.

Objective: "I can identify errors when commas are used to separate adjectives and can use a comma to separate coordinate adjectives correctly in my own writing."

Agenda:

1. Bell-ringer: Magic Lens Sentence Analysis—Since we are on level one of grammar study, TSW analyze a sentence for level one (the parts of speech) only.
2. Mini-Lesson: Adjectives—TSW take Cornell notes on adjectives including articles, the three degrees of adjectives, and coordinate vs. cumulative adjectives.
3. Read Aloud—TTW read an example of a SC Ready released test item that asks students to know the difference between coordinate and cumulative adjectives in order choose the correctly punctuated sentence. TSW discuss how this skill might be assessed through multiple choice responses and how they can also apply it to their writing.
4. Independent Practice—TSW complete a practice on adjectives on www.noredink.com.
5. Writing Workshop—TSW take out a piece of completed writing such a their letter to the teacher from the first week of school, highlight all commas used in the piece, edit their writing for correct comma usage using the new rule that was introduced, and add in at least one sentence using commas in a series to separate coordinate adjectives correctly.
6. Sharing/Closing—Each student will share the sentence he or she added to their letter to a Padlet, and the class will discuss.

Teaching as Language Evolves

Language, indeed, evolves over time, and as a result, some grammatical constructions do change. However, there are also some irrefutable facts of Standard American English Grammar that do not change, as noted in Appendix B. Teachers should "start teaching grammar, punctuation, and usage. Require students to memorize rules, pronoun charts, and lists of prepositions and conjunctions."[278] Once students have a foundational knowledge of the levels of grammar, they will be ready to discuss how language changes and evolves in higher-level English courses.

Grammar knowledge is not contrary to creativity; instead, the knowledge of the four levels of grammar provides the power for students to be able to enhance their creativity.

While an English teacher should be an expert in the structure of the English language, he or she should be viewed as "a guide and not a god or goddess."[279] Teachers should not be afraid to model their thinking in front of students. It is okay not to know all of the answers, as even experts do not always know every answer, but what is not okay is to give up puzzling over the complexity of the English language. It is also encouraged that the study of grammar goes beyond memorization of the irrefutable facts and on to creative license. "Grammar isn't about linguistic straight jackets and rules; it is how creativity manifests itself in language. Grammar is how we organize our words and sentences to communicate with others and to express ourselves."[280] Teachers have to move beyond the ideology that memorizing grammar facts is enough. Grammar teaching should be viewed as a means to an end—improved literacy, including improved academic writing skills—not the end itself.[281] Grammar knowledge is not contrary to creativity; instead, the knowledge of the four levels of grammar provides the power for students to be able to enhance their creativity.

Modernizing Resources

Grammar teaching has to move beyond where it once was before it was banned—skill and drill of facts with no application.

Grammar teaching has to move beyond where it once was before it was banned—skill and drill of facts with no application. In the past, "grammar instruction thrilled a few, bored most, and made no difference to reading and writing outcomes."[282] Teachers should limit the use of worksheets and grammar workbooks and move toward more engaging resources and activities. Four-level sentence analysis should be a common classroom practice and can be done in isolation as a warm-up activity or embedded within the study of writing and literature. Students should be challenged to approach all texts as literary critics, constantly examining the grammatical

choices of the authors they are reading. I also encourage teachers to utilize online resources such as www.noredink.com, which tailors questions to student interests while still reinforcing content.

The Writing Process and Grammar

Another suggestion is to teach the writing process, including prewriting, drafting, revising, editing, and publishing. Revising should focus on content, the development of ideas, organization, sentence fluency, and word choice. Editing should focus on proofreading for conventions such as spelling, grammar, punctuation, and capitalization. "Telling [students] to revise [isn't] enough… Writers need to arrange their ideas in some logical order that readers can follow. In order to arrange ideas, though, they need to identify how their ideas relate to one another. And in order to identify these relationships, they need to distinguish between main ideas and supporting details."[283] Students should be directed to use their knowledge of the levels of grammar for both revising and editing. For example, students can make choices as writers when revising for sentence fluency and word choice by determining what sentence structure to utilize based on the importance of the ideas within each clause. See Figure 5.4 for more details on the integration of grammar into the writing process.

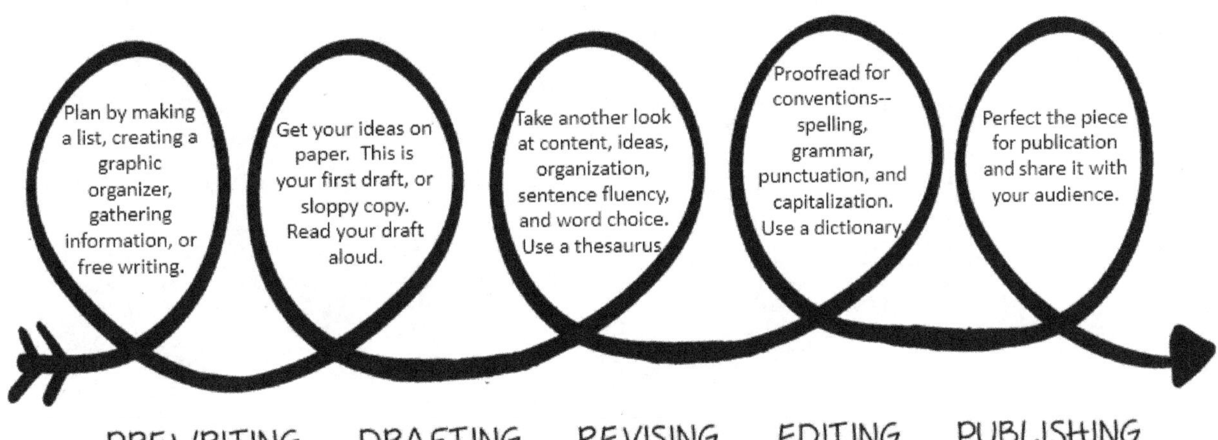

Figure 5.4. Image Showing the Integration of Grammar into the Writing Process

Listen to the Professionals Who Are in the Trenches

Many practicing teachers who are in the trenches day in and day out do not agree with the bulk of educational research on the subject of teaching grammar, but nobody is listening to their voices. We must encourage expert teachers to engage in more classroom action research in order to show the effectiveness of grammar teaching and to balance out the overwhelming amount of biased research against the practice that currently pervades databases. In the article, "How to Teach Grammar, Analytical Thinking, and Writing: A Method that Works" (2003), author Lynn Sams advocated:

> We need to free ourselves from the tendency to value research over the experience of the expert teacher. Methods that have been proven to work over time by teachers who know how to use them should not be summarily dismissed. Most importantly, care should be taken to align instructional methods with the nature of subject matter. In composition instruction, this leads to a classroom where grammar and writing are virtually inseparable.[284]

In a recent professional development, I heard a district leader tell a room full of teachers, "This presentation is based on real research—not just someone's classroom action research." Statements such as these not only devalue the expert opinions of teachers, but they also minimize the student achievement that supports teacher researchers' claims and discourage any future classroom action research. We must move away from attitudes that fail to recognize the experience and expertise of the professionals that we have hired to teach!

Chapter 6

Advice for Teachers on How to Teach Writing

Quarterly Learning Targets

My recommendation is that teachers teach writing in units just like they teach grammar in units. Each nine weeks, the teacher should reinforce what was taught in the grammar unit during the writing unit and expect students to show a mastery of those skills in their writing. This is not to say that grammar and writing are only taught in isolation. Grammar is like breathing in, and writing is like breathing out. Students need to learn the structure of their language so they can use it to craft written communication.

> *Grammar is like breathing in, and writing is like breathing out.*

In a sixty-minute class period, teachers can create a Writing Workshop that will introduce new content, reinforce prior learning, and allow time for conferencing. It is important to note that there should be a focused mini-lesson each day so that students are constantly being exposed to new learning. Here is a sample schedule for a class.

- **Bell-ringer (5 minutes)**—Magic Lens Sentence Analysis: Guide the students through the analysis of one sentence for each of the four levels of grammar that they have learned so far in the year. This is a great time for the teacher to model his or her own thinking about language and to encourage students to take the reins in leading that discussion.
- **Mini-Lesson (15 minutes)**—Direct instruction and focused note taking on a single topic/standard: Think about what students need to know to craft a well-written piece in the genre you are studying, and spend some time each day teaching those skills.
- **Read Aloud or Shared Writing (5 minutes)**—Read a portion of your own writing, a student exemplar, or a published work that demonstrates the standard you just taught. Build text sets for each writing study to use for this. Model your own writing process. Demonstrate your expectations.

- **Independent Practice (10 minutes)**—Students practice the skill in either isolation or in the context of reading or writing.
- **Writing Workshop Time (20 minutes)**—Students write as you conference with individuals and small groups. Take a status of the class during this time—a quick check-in to find out where each student is in the writing process.
- **Sharing and Closing (5 minutes)**—Writers read a portion of what they have written and seek feedback from their audience which can be a partner, a small group, or the whole group. You can share your writing, too. Have students target their feedback based on the rubric you will use to grade this type of writing.

Ninety-minute class periods simply allow more time for independent practice and Writing Workshop.

First Nine Weeks—The Parts of Speech and Narrative Writing

I recommend teaching narrative writing during the first nine weeks of school because of the ability for students and teachers to connect through shared experience. Whether students are writing a memoir or a personal narrative, teachers are able to get insight into their personal experiences and learn about them as individuals. Because writing about what you know is the easiest place to start, beginning with narrative writing allows students to build confidence as writers so that they can progress to more difficult genres during the year.

In a two-week unit on narrative writing, mini-lessons should include topics and essential questions such as:

- Establishing a clear setting (1 day)
  - When and where did the story take place?
- 1st person narrator (1 day)
  - How can I develop my voice as the protagonist of my story?
- Plot structure (1 day)
  - How can I include plot complications, a climax, and a resolution to craft my story?
- Chronological order and transition words (1 day)
- Effective opening (1 day)
  - How can I hook the reader's attention from the very first line?
  - Types of hooks include shocker, summary, dialogue, definition, problem, question, quotation, statement of authority, imagine

statement, imagery, and staccato three word lead. Which of these suits my story best?

  - How can I give just enough detail in my opening to make readers want to continue without spoiling all of the suspense?

- ❍ Building the body of the story through details, dialogue, and description (1 day)
  - How can I use prior knowledge about punctuating dialogue to convey conversations as they happened between characters?
  - How can I show the readers what happened instead of just telling them, so that they feel as if they are present in the moment?
  - How can I recreate what I was seeing, hearing, smelling, tasting, and touching or feeling through my words?
- ❍ Improving voice through sensory language, figurative language, and precise language (3 days)
  - How can I use specific nouns and vivid verbs in order to give readers an accurate mental image or exactly what I am describing?
  - How can I use action verbs as speech tag words other than said to convey how characters and communicating with each other?
  - How can I use pronouns to avoid repetition of character names?
  - How can I use adjectives and adverbs to add more detail to my story?
- ❍ Effective closing (1 day)
  - Why did I choose this topic, and what did I learn from this experience?
  - Why was my experience so great that I cannot forget it or so bad that I wish I could forget it?

Second Nine Weeks—The Parts of the Sentence and Phrases and Informational Writing

In the second nine weeks, it will be important to continue a spiral review so that students are aware that the skills learned during the first nine weeks should continue to be employed. Students should continue to work toward hooking the reader, using transitional devices, adding details and description, using precise language, and providing an effective conclusion. In a two-week unit on informational or explanatory writing, new mini-lessons should include topics and essential questions such as:

- Author's purpose and awareness of the audience (1 day)
  - — What is the difference between writing to persuade, to inform, or to entertain?
  - — Who is my target audience, and how can I tailor my writing to them?
  - — When it is appropriate for the narrator to use 2nd person point of view to speak directly to the reader?
- Staying on topic (1 day)
  - — How can I include supporting details that support the main idea?
  - — How can I avoid irrelevant details?
- Organization (1 day)
  - — How can I ensure that my writing has a clear beginning, middle, and end?
  - — How can I transition between sentences and between paragraphs effectively?
- Using the parts of the sentence (1 day)
  - — How can I use a balance of action verb and linking verb sentences in order to vary my sentence structures?
  - — How can I avoid inappropriate verb tense shifts?
- Using phrases to add depth and clarity to informational writing making it more engaging and informative to readers (6 days)
  - — How can I use appositives to provide additional information or clarification about a noun?
    - ◆ Example: My cousin's boyfriend, a talented guitarist, is the opening act at the show tonight.
  - — How can I use adjectival phrases to add specificity and detail to nouns?
    - ◆ Example: The ancient city, buried beneath centuries of ruins, was a geographical wonder.
  - — How can I use adverbial phrases to modify verbs, adjective, or other adverbs, providing even more nuance about how, when, where, or why something occurred.
    - ◆ Example: The boy crept toward the edge of the diving board, courageously facing his greatest fear.

- How can I use prepositional phrases to provide additional context or detail about location, time, or manner?
  - Example: In the heart of the forest, there is a quaint cottage reminiscent of a fairy tale.
- How can I use participial phrases to add action and variety to my writing?
  - Example: Waiting until the very last minute, Kevin reluctantly pulled out his notes and began to study for the exam.
- How can I use gerund phrases to discuss actions or activities as nouns?
  - Example: Eating dessert is something that I enjoy but don't do often.
- How can I use infinitive phrases to express purpose or intention?
  - Example: To improve her skills, Melissa joined a private volleyball club off season.

Third Nine Weeks—Clauses and Argumentative Writing

In the third nine weeks, students should be expected to show mastery of the skills learned during both first and second nine weeks in their writing. During this quarter, students will learn the art of argument. In a two-week unit on argumentative writing, new mini-lessons should include topics and essential questions such as:

- Making a claim (1 day)
  - What is the difference between an objective summary and an argumentative essay?
  - How can I stay on topic by arguing in favor of one viewpoint and refuting the opposite viewpoint?
- Crafting a thesis sentence (1 day)
  - How can I create a thesis that contains my claim and three supporting reasons with my strongest reason last?
  - How does this thesis statement set up the organization of the paper?
    - Reason number one becomes my first body paragraph.
    - Reason number two becomes my next body paragraph.
    - Reason number three becomes my third body paragraph leaving my strongest argument in the readers' minds.

- ❍ Citing relevant, textual evidence (1 day)
  - — How can I distinguish between fact and opinion in a source?
  - — How can I use paraphrases, direct quotation, and in-text citations to show proper attribution to authors?
- ❍ Organizing your essay (1 day)
  - — How can I include an introduction, body, rebuttal, and conclusion in my essay?
  - — See the Argumentative Essay Graphic Organizer in Appendix E.
- ❍ Varying sentence structure in your writing (3 days)
  - — How can I use a variety of sentence structures in my writing, so that no more than 50% of my sentences are simple?
  - — How can I combine simple sentences into either compound or complex sentences?
  - — How can I use commas and coordinating conjunctions or semi-colons to create compound sentences?
    - ◆ Example: Many people believe that writing is an art, but others claim that it is a science.
    - ◆ Example: Writing is an art; it is also a science.
  - — How can I use commas and subordinating conjunctions to create complex sentences?
    - ◆ Example: While many people would argue that writing is a science, I believe that it is more of an art.
  - — How can I determine as a writer the significance of each clause so that I can choose between a compound sentence where both clauses have equal importance or a complex sentence where one clause is dependent and therefore less significant than the independent clause?
- ❍ Acknowledging and refuting counterclaims (2 days)
  - — How can I craft a rebuttal paragraph that shows that I understand the opposing viewpoint and valid arguments associated with it?
  - — How can I acknowledge these claims, refute weak logic, and provide counterclaims to support my own stance?
  - — How can I maintain a respectful tone while engaging in the art of argument?

- Writing a conclusion (1 day)
  - How can I restate my thesis in a slightly different way in the conclusion?
  - How can I summarize my key points and call the readers to action?
  - How can I craft a memorable closing sentence?

Fourth Nine Weeks—All Four Levels of Grammar and Literary Analysis

Perhaps, the most difficult type of writing for students is that of literary analysis because often, the focus of the writer has to shift from the character to the author. In fact, many students go wrong with standardized writing prompts because they fail to make this shift of focus when the prompt they are given requires it. For that reason, I recommend teaching this type of writing during the last quarter of the school year after students have been exposed to all four levels of grammar and to narrative, informative, and argumentative writing. In the fourth nine weeks, students should be expected to show mastery of the skills learned during the first through third nine weeks in their writing. In a two-week unit on writing a literary analysis, new mini-lessons should include topics and essential questions such as:

- Deconstructing a writing prompt (1 day)
  - What am I being asked to do in the prompt, and on whom or what should I focus?
    - Example: One recurring them in *The Tragedy of Romeo and Juliet* is that hasty, reckless actions may have disastrous consequences. How does the author develop this theme throughout the drama? (Note: Based on this prompt, a student's essay should focus primarily on William Shakespeare and his creative choices, not on Romeo and his haste.)
- Review of author's craft (1 day)
  - How can I use what I have learned about an author's craft to read a text like a writer? (Examples of author's craft can include foreshadowing, irony, figurative language, allusion, characterization, dialogue, plot development, point of view, word choice and even grammatical choices such as sentence structure.)
- Crafting a thesis statement (1 day)
  - How can I create a focused thesis statement in which my claim clearly portrays my main argument or interpretation of the text?
  - When appropriate and specified by a writing prompt, how can I ensure that my thesis statement includes three areas of author's craft

or three examples of an author's choices to convey a theme, advance the plot, build suspense, or develop characters?

- ❍ Organizing your essay (1 day)
  - — How can I organize my essay into a clear beginning, middle, and end that will effectively address at least three areas of author's craft?
- ❍ Close reading and citing relevant, textual evidence (2 days)
  - — How can I read a text thoroughly annotating examples of relevant textual evidence that can support my claim?
  - — How can I utilize the historical, cultural, or social context of what I am reading in order to better understand it?
  - — How can I support my analysis with relevant textual evidence such as examples of instances of an author's stylistic choices?
- ❍ Explaining your evidence (1 day)
  - — How can I use the RACE Strategy to support my evidence by analyzing each direct quotation in detail, explaining how it contributes to the overall meaning of or effect on the text?
  - — See the RACE Strategy in Appendix F.
- ❍ Using punctuation (3 days)
  - — How can I use grade-level punctuation such as a semi-colon, a dash, and an ellipsis correctly? (Note: The types of punctuation will vary based on grade-level standards.)
  - — How can I punctuate compound and complex sentences correctly?
  - — How can I use quotation marks and parentheses to craft direct quotes and in-text citations?

Revisiting Revision and the Use of Artificial Intelligence (AI)

Artificial intelligence is not just the future; it's already here and can be incredibly useful for students when revising and editing.

It is important for students to learn to edit and revise their writing to improve clarity, coherence, and overall effectiveness of expression. Students should be encouraged to think about the traits of good writing such as the content and development of ideas, organization, word choice, voice, sentence fluency, and conventions when revising and editing. Students must also be taught that there is a difference between revising and editing. As stated in chapter 5, revising focuses on content while editing focuses on conventions.

REVISING	EDITING
When revising, writers analyze their writing for CONTENT.	When editing, writers analyze their writing for CONVENTIONS.
• Writing Traits: ✓ Ideas ✓ Organization ✓ Word Choice ✓ Voice	• Writing Traits: ✓ Sentence Fluency ✓ Conventions
• Tools Needed: ✓ Thesaurus ✓ Highlighters	• Tools Needed: ✓ Dictionary ✓ Red Pen

Figure 6.1. The Difference between Revising and Editing

Artificial intelligence is not just the future; it's already here and can be incredibly useful for students when revising and editing. Students and teachers alike are already using it, so educators need to teach students how to use it responsibly and harness its power for their good. I recommend introducing an AI tool such as ChatGPT to students during the revising and editing process. Students can give AI a command followed by a copy of their essay or a portion of their essay. Here are some examples of commands that can be used:

- Read the following essay and give me suggestions to improve it in each of the following areas: content and development of ideas, organization, word choice, voice, sentence fluency, and conventions.
- Analyze the following text sentence by sentence and provide an accurate count of how many simple, compound, and complex sentences it contains.
- Read the body of my essay and suggest some smoother transitions.
- I am concerned about the flow of my argument. Can you identify any weak points in my reasoning and suggest ways to strengthen it?
- Can you provide feedback on the tone of my essay and make suggestions to improve it?

- I am required to use an ellipsis, a dash, a semi-colon, and quotation marks correctly in my essay. Can you tell me if I have achieved this and if I have made any errors with these types of punctuation?
- Can you help me identify any grammar and punctuation errors?
- Can you check to see if I have quoted and cited from sources correctly?

Teachers have always taught students how to avoid plagiarism when quoting from a source. Likewise, it is imperative that teachers model for students how to take suggestions from AI without copying and pasting so that the writer's voice and originality is still present within the text. Students should be exposed to plagiarism checkers and should be taught tips and tricks to check themselves. For example, it there are any words in your essay that you cannot pronounce or define, there is a problem.

In addition to providing automated feedback and revision suggestions to students, AI is also useful to classroom teachers because it can be used to detect plagiarism, to generate writing prompts, to help teachers with their grading workload, and even to translate content into other languages for students. By integrating AI into the processes of teaching and learning, students and teachers can leverage technology to streamline the workflow and learning outcomes.

Key Takeaways for Teachers

If this book has been successful at convincing you that systematic grammar instruction can, in fact, improve the teaching and learning of writing, here are some key takeaways and action steps for you.

- **Recognize the Importance of Teacher Preparation:** Teacher preparation in grammar instruction is essential. Advocate for mandatory English grammar classes in teacher preparation programs to ensure educators have the necessary expertise.
- **Improve Teacher Attitudes:** Teacher attitudes toward teaching grammar significantly impact student outcomes. Work on improving your own background knowledge of and attitude towards grammar to better support student learning.
- **Plan Vertically:** Emphasize the need for systematic grammar teaching from Kindergarten through Grade 12. Develop a curriculum that gradually builds student competency in grammar over time.

- **Implement Systematic Grammar Instruction:** Adopt a systematic approach to teaching grammar, focusing on the four levels: parts of speech, the parts of the sentence, phrases, and clauses. Ensure that students have a solid foundational understanding before progressing to more complex concepts.

The Grammar Inquiry and System Teaching (GIST) Strategy guides pedagogy around grammar instruction. It emphasizes inquiry, learning as a complex system, and application to reading and writing.

- **Apply Grammar Content to Writing:** Move beyond error correction and focus on immediate application of grammar knowledge to writing. Encourage students to practice grammar skills through various writing activities and assignments. During grammar units, students should be required to write and/or analyze their own writing. During writing units, students should be required to use their grammatical skills.
- **Utilize the GIST Teaching Strategy:** The Grammar Inquiry and System Teaching (GIST) Strategy guides pedagogy around grammar instruction. It emphasizes inquiry, learning as a complex system, and application to reading and writing.
- **Teach Grammar and Writing in Units:** Break down both grammar and writing instruction into manageable units throughout the year. Incorporate grammar topics into daily lessons and provide ample opportunities for practice and application. Teach a unit on each of the four levels of grammar—the parts of speech, the parts of the sentence, phrases, and clauses. Organize each nine-week period around a specific writing focus, such as narrative, informational, argumentative, and literary analysis. This structured approach allows for focused instruction and gradual skill development. Encourage students to show mastery of grammar skills in each writing unit.
- **Teach the Writing Process:** Integrate grammar instruction into the writing process, emphasizing the importance of revising for content and editing for grammar conventions.
- **Incorporate Daily Mini-Lessons:** Incorporate daily mini-lessons and targeted instruction to introduce new skills and concepts. Ensure that each mini-lesson aligns with the broader writing objectives for the unit.
- **Implement Writing Workshop:** Create a Writing Workshop structure in your classroom that provides dedicated time for students to practice writing while receiving individualized support and feedback. During this time, teachers can conference with students, assess progress, and provide guidance on improving writing skills.

- **Modernize Resources:** Utilize engaging resources and activities to teach grammar, moving away from traditional skill and drill methods. Incorporate online platforms like NoRedInk to tailor grammar instruction to student interests.
- **Integrate Technology:** Introduce students to artificial intelligence (AI) tools like ChatGPT to support the revision and editing processes. Encourage students to use AI responsibly, leveraging its capabilities to enhance their writing while maintaining their original voice and creativity. Model how to integrate AI feedback effectively without relying solely on automated suggestions.
- **Educate Students on Plagiarism:** Help students understand plagiarism and the importance of maintaining originality in their writing. Teach strategies for avoiding plagiarism, such as proper citation and paraphrasing techniques. Use plagiarism checkers as tools to reinforce academic integrity and ensure the authenticity of student work.
- **Provide Continuous Assessment:** Regularly assess student progress and understanding throughout the writing process. Use formative assessments, peer feedback, writer's checklists, and rubrics to provide ongoing support and guidance. Adjust instruction based on student needs and areas for improvement identified through assessment data.

By implementing these strategies, teachers can create a supportive and structured learning environment that empowers students to develop strong writing skills. Through systematic instruction, consistent practice, daily application, and the integration of technology, students can become proficient writers capable of crafting effective written communication across various genres and contexts.

APPENDICES

Appendix A

The Four Levels of Grammar

Level One: The Eight Parts of Speech

1. noun
2. pronoun
3. adjective
4. verb
5. adverb
6. preposition
7. interjection
8. conjunction

Level Two: The Parts of a Sentence

- sentence
- fragment
- subject
- predicate
- action verb
- direct object
- indirect object
- linking verb
- subject complement
- predicate nominative
- predicate adjective

Level Three: Phrases

- ❍ phrase
- ❍ prepositional phrase
- ❍ appositive
- ❍ verbal phrase
- ❍ gerund and gerund phrase
- ❍ participle and participial phrase
- ❍ dangling modifier
- ❍ misplaced modifier
- ❍ infinitive and infinitive phrase
- ❍ split infinitive

Level Four: Clauses

- ❍ independent clause
- ❍ dependent clause
- ❍ sentence structure
- ❍ simple
- ❍ compound
- ❍ complex
- ❍ compound-complex
- ❍ sentence errors
- ❍ fragments
- ❍ run-on sentences
- ❍ comma splices
- ❍ sentence purposes
- ❍ declarative
- ❍ imperative
- ❍ interrogative
- ❍ exclamatory

Appendix B

The Irrefutable Facts of Standard American English Grammar

Level 1: The Eight Parts of Speech

There are only eight kinds of words in Standard American English.

The eight parts of speech include:

1. A **noun** is a person, place, thing, or idea.
2. A **pronoun** replaces a noun.
3. An **adjective** modifies a noun.
4. A **verb** is a word that shows action, being, or links a subject to its subject complement
5. An **adverb** modifies a verb, an adjective, or another adverb.
6. A **preposition** shows relationship between its object and another word in the sentence.
7. An **interjection** shows emotion but has no grammatical function.
8. A **conjunction** joins two words or groups of words.

Level 2: The Parts of a Sentence

A **sentence** is a group of words that has a subject and its predicate and makes a complete thought; however, a **fragment** is an incomplete sentence because it either lacks a subject, lacks a predicate, or fails to make a complete thought.

The parts of the sentence include:

- A **subject** is the noun or subject pronoun that the sentence is about.
- A **predicate** includes the verb and other words that are about the subject.
- An **action verb** shows action.
- **Intransitive** action verbs are not followed by any additional parts of the sentence.

- **Transitive** action verbs are followed by a direct object.
- A **direct object** is the noun or object pronoun that receives the action of a transitive action verb.
- An **indirect object** is the noun or object pronoun between the transitive action verb and the direct object that is indirectly affected by the action.
- A **linking verb** links the subject to a subject complement.
- A **subject complement** is the noun, subject pronoun, or adjective, that is linked to the subject by a linking verb and that tells more about the subject
- A subject complement is considered **predicate nominative** if the subject complement is a noun or subject pronoun.
- A subject complement is considered **predicate adjective** if the subject complement is an adjective

Level 3: Phrases

A **phrase** is a group of words without a subject and its predicate that acts like a single part of speech.

The types of phrases include:

- **A prepositional phrase** begins with a preposition, ends with an object, and acts as an adjective or adverb.
- An **appositive** is an interrupting definition.
- A **verbal** is a verb form used as a different part of speech. There are three types of verbals:
  - A **gerund** is a noun made from an –ing verb form.
  - A **participle** is an adjective made from any verb form.
    - **A dangling modifier** is an error with a participial phrase where the noun being modified is missing from the sentence.
    - A **misplaced modifier** is an error with a participial phrase where the noun being modified is in the wrong place in the sentence.
  - An **infinitive** is a noun or modifier made from the to- form of the verb.
    - A **split infinitive** is an error with an infinitive phrase where a word is incorrectly placed between "to" and the rest of the verb form.

Level 4: Clauses

There are two types of clauses, four sentence structures, and four sentence purposes.

- Each group of words containing a subject and predicate is called a **clause**.
- There are two types of clauses:
  - An **independent clause** can stand alone as a complete sentence.
  - A **dependent clause** needs to be connected to an independent clause in order to make sense.
- There are four sentence structures:
  - A **simple sentence** contains one independent clause.
  - A **compound sentence** contains two or more independent clauses that are joined together by either a semi-colon or a comma and coordinating conjunction.
  - A **complex sentence** contains one independent clause and one dependent clause joined by a subordinating conjunction.
  - A **compound-complex sentence** contains two independent clauses and one or more dependent clauses. It is a compound sentence and a complex sentence combined.
- There are four sentence purposes:
  - A **declarative sentence** makes a declaration or statement.
  - An **imperative sentence** gives a command.
  - An **interrogative sentence** asks a question.
  - An **exclamatory sentence** exclaims.

Appendix C

Vertical Planning Pacing Guide for English Language Arts Standards

Vertical Planning Pacing Guide for English Language Standards

Grammar Level 1: The Parts of Speech
Grammar Level 2: The Parts of the Sentence
Grammar Level 3: Phrases
Grammar Level 4: Clauses and Sentences
Conventions: Spelling, Punctuation, and Capitalization

Jennifer Roach

Table 1

	Grammar Level 1	Grammar Level 2	Grammar Level 3	Grammar Level 4	Conventions		
	The Parts of Speech	The Parts of the Sentence	Phrases	Clauses and Sentences	Spelling	Punctuation	Capitalization
KINDERGARTEN	• Nouns - Singular - Plural by adding /s/ or /es/ • Verbs • Adjectives • Prepositions • Conjunctions	• Complete Sentences	• Prepositional Phrases	• Interrogatives	• Write letters for familiar consonant and vowel sounds. • Spell simple words phonetically. • Consult resources to check and correct spelling.	• Recognize and name end punctuation.	• Capitalize the first word in a sentence and the pronoun *I*.
FIRST GRADE	• Nouns - Common - Proper - Possessive - Singular - Plural • Verbs • Adjectives • Adverbs • Pronouns - Personal - Possessive - Indefinite • Prepositions • Conjunctions	• Complete Sentences	· Prepositional Phrases	• Simple Sentences • Compound Sentences • Sentence Purposes - Declarative - Interrogative - Imperative - Exclamatory	• Use conventional spelling for words with common spelling patterns. • Spell unknown words phonetically. • Spell common irregularly-spelled, grade level words. • Consult resources to check and correct spelling.	• Use periods, question marks, or exclamation marks at the ends of sentences. • Use commas in dates and to separate items in a series.	• Capitalize the first word of a sentence, dates, names, and the pronoun *I*.
SECOND GRADE	• Nouns - Collective Nouns - Irregular Plural Nouns • Verbs - Past Tense of Irregular Verbs • Adjectives vs. Adverbs • Pronouns - Reflexive • Prepositions • Conjunctions	• Complete Sentences	• Prepositional Phrases - Positional - Time - Place	• Simple Sentences • Compound Sentences	• Generalize learned spelling patterns and word families. • Correctly spell words with short and long vowel sounds, r-controlled vowels, consonant-blend patterns, and common irregularly-spelled, grade level words. • Consult resources to check and correct spelling.	• Use periods, question marks, or exclamation marks at the ends of sentences. • Use commas in greetings and closings of letters, dates, and to separate items in a series. • Use apostrophes to form contractions and singular possessive nouns.	• Capitalize greetings, months, days of the week, holidays, geographic names, and titles.

Table 2

	Grammar Levels 1-2	Grammar Level 3	Grammar Level 4	Conventions		
	The Parts of Speech and The Parts of the Sentence	Phrases	Clauses and Sentences	Spelling	Punctuation	Capitalization
THIRD GRADE	• Nouns - Regular and Irregular Plurals - Abstract Nouns • Verbs - Regular and Irregular - Simple Verb Tense • Adjectives - Comparative, Superlative, and Coordinating • Adverbs • Pronouns - Pronoun/Antecedent Agreement • Prepositions • Conjunctions - Coordinating and Subordinating • Subject/Verb Agreement	• Prepositional Phrases	• Simple Sentences • Compound Sentences • Complex Sentences	• Use conventional spelling for high-frequency words, previously studied words, and for adding suffixes to base words. • Use spelling patterns and generalizations. • Consult resources to check and correct spellings.	• Use apostrophes to form contractions and singular possessive nouns. • Use quotation marks to mark and direct speech. • Use commas in locations and addresses, to mark and direct speech, and with coordinating adjectives.	• Capitalize appropriate words in titles, historical periods, company names, product names, and special events.
FOURTH GRADE	• Nouns • Verbs - Progressive Verb Tense - Modal Auxiliaries to convey various conditions - Correcting inappropriate shifts in tense • Adjectives - Ordering adjectives • Adverbs - Relative Adverbs • Pronouns - Relative Pronouns • Prepositions • Conjunctions - Coordinating and Subordinating • Complete Sentences	• Prepositional Phrases in various positions in the sentence	• Simple Sentences • Compound Sentences • Complex Sentences • Correcting Sentence Fragments and Run-ons	• Use conventional spelling for high-frequency words, previously studied words, and for adding suffixes to base words. • Use spelling patterns and generalizations. • Consult resources to check and correct spellings.	• Use apostrophes to form contractions and possessives. • Use quotation marks and commas to direct speech. • Use a comma before a coordinating conjunction in a compound sentence.	• Capitalize names of magazines, newspapers, works of art, musical compositions, organizations, and the first word in quotations, when appropriate.

Table 3

	Grammar Levels 1-2 The Parts of Speech and The Parts of the Sentence	Grammar Level 3 Phrases	Grammar Level 4 Clauses and Sentences	Conventions Spelling	 Punctuation	 Capitalization
FIFTH GRADE	• Nouns • Verbs - Perfect Verb Tense - Use verb tense to convey time, sequence, state, or condition - Correcting inappropriate shifts in tense • Adjectives • Adverbs • Pronouns • Prepositions • Conjunctions - Coordinating, Subordinating, and Correlative • Interjections • Complete Sentences	• Prepositional Phrases • Appositives	• Simple Sentences • Compound Sentences • Complex Sentence • Correcting Sentence Fragments and Run-ons	• Use conventional spelling for high-frequency words, previously studied words, and for adding suffixes to base words. • Use spelling patterns and generalizations. • Consult resources to check and correct spellings.	• Use apostrophes and quotation marks. • Use commas for appositives, to set off the words *yes* and *no*, to set off a tag question from the rest of the sentence, and to indicate direct address. • Use a comma before a coordinating conjunction in a compound sentence.	• Apply correct usage of capitalization in writing.
SIXTH GRADE	• Nouns • Verbs • Adjectives • Adverbs • Pronouns - Pronoun Case: Subjective, Objective, and Possessive - Intensive Pronouns - Recognize shifts in pronoun number and person - Correct unclear/ambiguous antecedents • Prepositions • Conjunctions • Interjections • Subjects • Action Verbs • Direct Objects • Indirect Objects • Linking Verbs • Subject Complements	• Prepositional Phrases • Appositives • Verbal Phrases - Gerund Phrases - Infinitive Phrases - Participial Phrases	• Independent Clauses • Dependent Clauses • Simple Sentences • Compound Sentences • Complex Sentences • Correcting Sentence Fragments and Run-ons	• Use conventional spelling for high-frequency words, previously studied words, and for adding suffixes to base words. • Use spelling patterns and generalizations. • Consult resources to check and correct spellings.	• Use commas, parentheses, and dashes to set off nonrestrictive/parenthetical elements. • Use semicolons to connect main clauses. • Use colons to introduce a list or quotation. • Use a comma before a coordinating conjunction in a compound sentence.	• Apply correct usage of capitalization in writing.

Table 4

	Grammar Levels 1-2	Grammar Level 3	Grammar Level 4	Conventions		
	The Parts of Speech and The Parts of the Sentence	Phrases	Clauses and Sentences	Spelling	Punctuation	Capitalization
SEVENTH GRADE	• Nouns • Verbs • Adjectives • Adverbs - Coordinate Adjectives vs. Cumulative Adjectives • Pronouns • Prepositions • Conjunctions • Interjections • Subjects • Action Verbs • Direct Objects • Indirect Objects • Linking Verbs • Subject Complements	• Prepositional Phrases • Appositives • Verbal Phrases - Gerund Phrases - Infinitive Phrases - Participial Phrases • Correcting Misplaced and Dangling Modifiers • Correcting Split Infinitives	• Independent Clauses • Dependent Clauses • Simple Sentences • Compound Sentences • Complex Sentences • Compound-Complex Sentences • Correcting Sentence Fragments and Run-ons	• Use conventional spelling for high-frequency words, previously studied words, and for adding suffixes to base words. • Use spelling patterns and generalizations. • Consult resources to check and correct spellings.	• Use commas to separate coordinate adjectives. • Use a comma before a coordinating conjunction in a compound sentence. • Use commas after introductory subordinate clauses (such as in complex sentences).	• Apply correct usage of capitalization in writing.
EIGHTH GRADE	• Nouns • Verbs - Active and Passive Verbs - Verb Moods:Indicative, Imperative, Interrogative, Subjunctive, and Conditional - Correct inappropriate shifts in voice and mood • Adjectives • Adverbs • Pronouns • Prepositions • Conjunctions • Interjections • Subjects • Action Verbs • Direct Objects • Indirect Objects • Linking Verbs • Subject Complements	• Prepositional Phrases • Appositives • Verbal Phrases - Gerunds as Nouns - Infinitives as Nouns, Adjectives, or Adverbs - Participles as Adjectives • Correcting Misplaced and Dangling Modifiers • Correcting Split Infinitives	• Independent Clauses • Dependent Clauses • Simple Sentences • Compound Sentences • Complex Sentences • Compound-Complex Sentences • Correcting Sentence Fragments and Run-ons	• Use conventional spelling for high-frequency words, previously studied words, and for adding suffixes to base words. • Use spelling patterns and generalizations. • Consult resources to check and correct spellings.	• Use commas, ellipses, and dashes to indicate a pause, a break, or an omission. • Use a comma before a coordinating conjunction in a compound sentence. • Use commas after introductory subordinate clauses (such as in complex sentences).	• Apply correct usage of capitalization in writing.

Table 5

	Grammar Levels 1-2	Grammar Level 3	Grammar Level 4	Conventions		
	The Parts of Speech and The Parts of the Sentence	Phrases	Clauses and Sentences	Spelling	Punctuation	Capitalization
ENGLISH 1	• Parallel Structure • Verbs - Active and Passive Verbs - Verb Moods: Indicative, Imperative, Interrogative, Subjunctive, and Conditional • Adverbs - Conjunctive Adverbs	• Noun Phrases • Verbal Phrases - Gerunds as Nouns - Infinitives as Nouns, Adjectives, or Adverbs - Participles as Adjectives • Adjectival Phrases • Adverbial Phrases • Prepositional Phrases • Absolute Phrases	• Independent Clauses • Dependent Clauses • Noun Clauses • Relative Clauses • Adverbial Clauses	• Use conventional spelling for high-frequency words, previously studied words, and for adding suffixes to base words. • Use spelling patterns and generalizations. • Consult resources to check and correct spellings.	• Use a semi-colon or a subjunctive adverb to link independent clauses. • Use a colon to introduce a list or quotation. • Use commas to separate adjacent, parallel structures. • Use a comma before a coordinating conjunction in a compound sentence. • Use commas after introductory subordinate clauses (such as in complex	• Apply correct usage of capitalization in writing.
ENGLISH 2	• Parallel Structure	• Noun Phrases • Verbal Phrases - Gerund as Nouns - Infinitives as Nouns, Adjectives, or Adverbs - Participles as Adjectives • Adjectival Phrases • Adverbial Phrases • Prepositional Phrases • Absolute Phrases	• Independent Clauses • Dependent Clauses • Noun Clauses • Relative Clauses • Adverbial Clauses	• Use conventional spelling for high-frequency words, previously studied words, and for adding suffixes to base words. • Use spelling patterns and generalizations. • Consult resources to check and correct spellings.	• Use a semi-colon or a subjunctive adverb to link independent clauses. • Use a colon to introduce a list or quotation. • Use commas to separate adjacent, parallel structures. • Use a comma before a coordinating conjunction in a compound sentence. • Use commas after introductory subordinate clauses (such as in complex	• Apply correct usage of capitalization in writing.

Table 6

<table>
<tr><th rowspan="2"></th><th rowspan="2"></th><th>Grammar Level 3</th><th>Grammar Level 4</th><th colspan="3">Conventions</th></tr>
<tr><th>Phrases</th><th>Clauses and Sentences</th><th>Spelling</th><th>Punctuation</th><th>Capitalization</th></tr>
<tr><td rowspan="2">ENGLISH 3</td><td rowspan="2">• Apply the understanding that usage is a matter of convention, can change over time, and is sometimes contested.
• Resolve issues of complex or contested usage, consulting references as needed.</td><td rowspan="2">• Noun Phrases
• Verbal Phrases
- Gerunds as Nouns
- Infinitives as Nouns, Adjectives, or Adverbs
- Participles as Adjectives
• Adjectival Phrases
• Adverbial Phrases
• Prepositional Phrases
• Absolute Phrases</td><td rowspan="2">• Independent Clauses
• Dependent Clauses
• Noun Clauses
• Relative Clauses
• Adverbial Clauses</td><td colspan="3">• Demonstrate a command of the conventions of Standard English capitalization, punctuation, and spelling.</td></tr>
<tr><td>• Use conventional spelling for high-frequency words, previously studied words, and for adding suffixes to base words.
• Use spelling patterns and generalizations.
• Consult resources to check and correct spellings.</td><td>• Mastery of the following:
- Semicolon
- Colon
- Comma
- Hyphenation
• Use a comma before a
• Use a comma before a coordinating conjunction in a compound sentence.
• Use commas after introductory subordinate clauses (such as in complex sentences).</td><td>• Apply correct usage of capitalization in writing.</td></tr>
<tr><td rowspan="2">ENGLISH 4</td><td rowspan="2">• Apply the understanding that usage is a matter of convention, can change over time, and is sometimes contested.
• Resolve issues of complex or contested usage, consulting references as needed.</td><td rowspan="2">• Noun Phrases
• Verbal Phrases
- Gerund as Nouns
- Infinitives as Nouns, Adjectives, or Adverbs
- Participles as Adjectives
• Adjectival Phrases
• Adverbial Phrases
• Prepositional Phrases
• Absolute Phrases</td><td rowspan="2">• Independent Clauses
• Dependent Clauses
• Noun Clauses
• Relative Clauses
• Adverbial Clauses</td><td colspan="3">• Demonstrate a command of the conventions of Standard English capitalization, punctuation, and spelling.</td></tr>
<tr><td>• Use conventional spelling for high-frequency words, previously studied words, and for adding suffixes to base words.
• Use spelling patterns and generalizations.
• Consult resources to check and correct spellings.</td><td>• Use a comma before a coordinating conjunction in a compound sentence.
• Use commas after introductory subordinate clauses (such as in complex sentences).</td><td>• Apply correct usage of capitalization in writing.</td></tr>
</table>

Appendix D

The GIST Strategy: Helping Students Get the "Gist" of the English Language

GIST

Grammar Inquiry and System Teaching

Grammar must be discovered through inquiry, taught as a complex system, and applied to reading and writing!

INQUIRE	LEARN	APPLY
Inquiry into Grammatical Structures and Choices	Learning Grammar as a Complex System	Application of Grammar to Reading and Writing
Students acquire implicit knowledge of grammatical constructions by thinking about language. Students analyze authors' choices in style, usage, and syntax. Students evaluate their own choices as writers.	Students build their explicit knowledge of syntax by learning the four levels of grammar that build on each other and form a complex system—the parts of speech, the parts of the sentence, phrases, and clauses. They practice four-level sentence analysis and sentence combining.	Students apply their learning to their reading, writing, and speaking. They form more complex sentence structures in their writing. They use punctuation as a function of grammar. They use the levels of grammar to identify the main idea of each sentence that they read and write.

The Parts of Speech . The Parts of the Sentence . Phrases . Clauses

APPENDIX E

Argumentative Essay Graphic Organizer

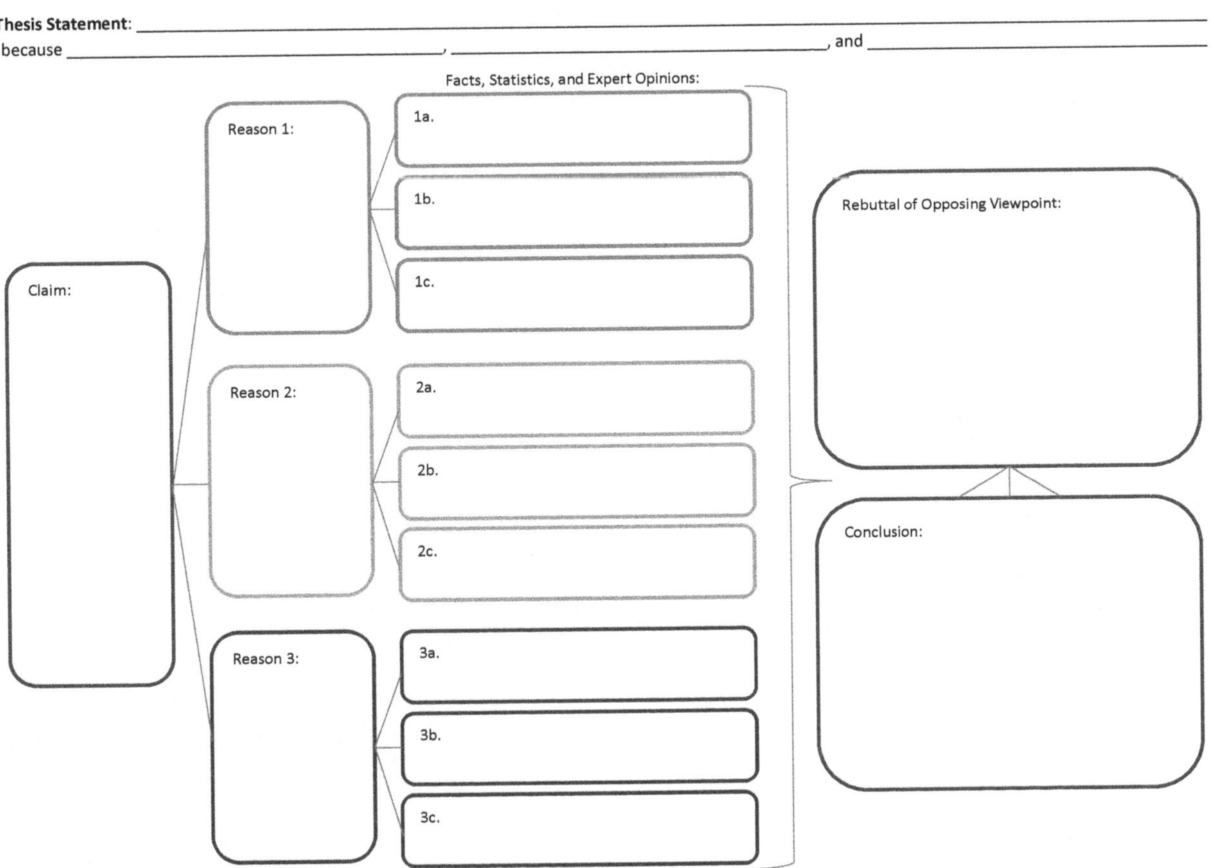

The RACE Strategy

RACE Strategy

R – Restate the question with any keywords.

A – Answer the question with an evidence based term.

C – Cite support from the text using an in-text citation.

E – Explain the significance of your evidence.

Endnotes

[1] Thompson, Michael C. *The Verbal Option.* Understanding Our Gifted 14, no. 1 (2001): 7-10.

[2] Goldstein, Dana. "Why Kids Can›t Write." *The New York Times*, August 2, 2017.

[3] Goldstein, Dana. "Why Kids Can›t Write." *The New York Times*, August 2, 2017.

[4] Buerke, Amanda M. "Relationship between Traditional Grammar Terminology and Metacognitive Application of Grammar Concepts." Master of Education Program Theses, Dordt University, 2005.

[5] Goldstein, Dana. "Why Kids Can't Write." *The New York Times*, August 2, 2017.

[6] Boumova, Vera. "Traditional vs. Modern Teaching Methods: Advantages and Disadvantages of Each." Masaryk University, 2008.

[7] Goldstein, Dana. "Why Kids Can't Write." *The New York Times*, August 2, 2017.

[8] Blystone, Stephen M. "Caught in the Grammar Crossfire: One Student's Plea and Plan for Peace." *Issue in Writing* 12, no. 1 (2001): 24-42.

[9] Blystone, Stephen M. "Caught in the Grammar Crossfire: One Student's Plea and Plan for Peace." *Issue in Writing* 12, no. 1 (2001): 24-42.

[10] Thompson, Michael C. *Four-Level Grammar and Academic Writing.* Unionville, NY: Royal Fireworks Press, n.d.

[11] Neuleib, Janice, and Linda Brosnahan. "Teaching Grammar to Writers." *Journal of Basic Writing* 6, no. 1 (1987): 28-35.

[12] Neuleib, Janice, and Linda Brosnahan. "Teaching Grammar to Writers." *Journal of Basic Writing* 6, no. 1 (1987): 28-35.

[13] Neuleib, Janice, and Linda Brosnahan. "Teaching Grammar to Writers." *Journal of Basic Writing* 6, no. 1 (1987): 28-35.

[14] Neuleib, Janice, and Linda Brosnahan. "Teaching Grammar to Writers." *Journal of Basic Writing* 6, no. 1 (1987): 28-35.

[15] Vavra, Ed. "On Not Teaching Grammar." *The English Journal* 85, no. 7 (1996): 32-37.

[16] Vavra, Ed. "On Not Teaching Grammar." *The English Journal* 85, no. 7 (1996): 32-37.

[17] Thompson, Michael C. *Vocabulary and Grammar: Critical Content for Critical Thinking. Journal of Secondary Gifted Education* 13, no. 2 (2002): 60-66.

[18] Thompson, Michael C. *Vocabulary and Grammar: Critical Content for Critical Thinking. Journal of Secondary Gifted Education* 13, no. 2 (2002): 60-66.

[19] Graham, Steve, and Dolores Perin. *Writing Next: Effective Strategies to Improve Writing of Adolescents in Middle and High Schools.* Washington, D.C.: Alliance for Excellent Education, 2007.

[20] "Crisis Point: The State of Literacy in America." Blog post, March 5, 2018.

[21] Johnson, Andrew P. *Academic Writing: Process and Product.* Lanham, MD: Rowman & Littlefield, 2016.

[22] Thompson, Michael C. *Advanced Academic Writing. Volume 2.* Unionville, NY: Royal Fireworks Press, 2009.

[23] Lakhoua, Dhouha. "To Teach or Not to Teach Grammar: A Controversy?" Arab Open University, n.d.

[24] The Nation's Report Card Releases Results from an Innovative, Interactive Computer-Based Writing Assessment." Washington, DC: National Assessment Governing Board, 2011.

[25] Kuczynski-Brown, Alexandra. "Most U.S. Students Lack Writing Proficiency, National Assessment of Educational Progress Finds." *HuffPost*, 2012.

[26] Graham, Steve, and Dolores Perin. *Writing Next: Effective Strategies to Improve Writing of Adolescents in Middle and High Schools.* Washington, D.C.: Alliance for Excellent Education, 2007.

[27] Goldstein, Dana. "Why Kids Can›t Write." *The New York Times*, August 2, 2017.

[28] "The Decline of Students› Writing Skills: Causes and Outcomes." Blog post, August 5, 2015.

[29] Thompson, Michael C. *The Verbal Option.* Understanding Our Gifted 14, no. 1 (2001): 7-10.

[30] Camara, Wayne J., et al. *ACT Research Explains New ACT Test Writing Scores and Their Relationships to Other Test Scores.* Iowa City, Iowa: ACT, 2016.

[31] Camara, Wayne J., et al. *ACT Research Explains New ACT Test Writing Scores and Their Relationships to Other Test Scores.* Iowa City, Iowa: ACT, 2016.

[32] The Nation's Report Card Releases Results from an Innovative, Interactive Computer-Based Writing Assessment." Washington, DC: National Assessment Governing Board, 2011.

[33] Vavra, Ed. "On Not Teaching Grammar." *The English Journal* 85, no. 7 (1996): 32-37.

[34] Selingo, Jeffrey J. "Why Can't College Graduates Write Coherent Prose?" *The Washington Post*, August 11, 2017.

[35] The Decline of Students› Writing Skills: Causes and Outcomes." Blog post, August 5, 2015.

[36] Goldstein, Dana. "Why Kids Can›t Write." *The New York Times*, August 2, 2017.

[37] The ACT Profile Report: Graduating Class 2018—National." Iowa City, Iowa: ACT, 2018.

[38] The ACT Profile Report: Graduating Class 2018—National." Iowa City, Iowa: ACT, 2018.

[39] Selingo, Jeffrey J. "Why Can't College Graduates Write Coherent Prose?" *The Washington Post*, August 11, 2017.

[40] Selingo, Jeffrey J. "Why Can't College Graduates Write Coherent Prose?" *The Washington Post*, August 11, 2017.

[41] Graham, Steve, and Dolores Perin. *Writing Next: Effective Strategies to Improve Writing of Adolescents in Middle and High Schools.* Washington, D.C.: Alliance for Excellent Education, 2007.

[42] Graham, Steve, and Dolores Perin. *Writing Next: Effective Strategies to Improve Writing of Adolescents in Middle and High Schools.* Washington, D.C.: Alliance for Excellent Education, 2007.

[43] Thompson, Michael C. *Vocabulary and Grammar: Critical Content for Critical Thinking. Journal of Secondary Gifted Education* 13, no. 2 (2002): 60-66.

[44] Thompson, Michael C. *The Verbal Option.* Understanding Our Gifted 14, no. 1 (2001): 7-10.

[45] Thompson, Michael C. *The Verbal Option.* Understanding Our Gifted 14, no. 1 (2001): 7-10.

[46] Thompson, Michael C. *The Verbal Option.* Understanding Our Gifted 14, no. 1 (2001): 7-10.

[47] Singleton, Carl. "We Can Never Teach Students to Write If They Can't Use Standard Grammar." *Chronicle of Higher Education*, May 20, 1987, 40-41.

[48] Thompson, Michael C. *The Verbal Option.* Understanding Our Gifted 14, no. 1 (2001): 7-10.

[49] Thompson, Michael C. *Vocabulary and Grammar: Critical Content for Critical Thinking. Journal of Secondary Gifted Education* 13, no. 2 (2002): 60-66.

[50] Thompson, Michael C. *Vocabulary and Grammar: Critical Content for Critical Thinking. Journal of Secondary Gifted Education* 13, no. 2 (2002): 60-66.

[51] Thompson, Michael C. *The Magic Lens.* Vol. 2. Unionville, NY: Royal Fireworks Press, 2002, 9-10.

[52] Mulroy, David. *The War Against Grammar.* Portsmouth, NH: Boynton/Cook Publishers, 2003, xi.

[53] Singh, Ramjee. "Controversies in Teaching English Grammar." *Academic Voices: A Multi-disciplinary Journal* 1, no. 1 (2011): 56-60.

[54] Mulroy, David. *The War Against Grammar.* Portsmouth, NH: Boynton/Cook Publishers, 2003, 78.

[55] Mulroy, David. *The War Against Grammar.* Portsmouth, NH: Boynton/Cook Publishers, 2003, 43.

[56] Weaver, Constance. "Teaching Grammar in the Context of Writing." *The English Journal* 85, no. 7 (1996): 15-24.

57 Bentsen, Lise G. "To Teach, or Not to Teach Grammar? Teachers' Approaches to Grammar Teaching in Lower Secondary School." Master's thesis, Universitetet I Oslo, 2017.

58 Ravitch, Diane. "Subordinate Clause Without Any Pauses: Why We Need a Language With Some Lawses." *Education Next* 5, no. 2 (2005): 78-79.

59 Amare, Nicole. "Style: The New Grammar in Composition Studies?" In *Refiguring Prose Style: Possibilities for Writing Pedagogy*, edited by Theresa Johnson and Tom Pace, 153-66. University Press of Colorado, 2005. doi:10.2307/j.ctt4cgq34.17.

60 Mulroy, David. *The War Against Grammar*. Portsmouth, NH: Boynton/Cook Publishers, 2003, 60.

61 Mulroy, David. *The War Against Grammar*. Portsmouth, NH: Boynton/Cook Publishers, 2003, 60.

62 Weaver, Constance. "Teaching Grammar in the Context of Writing." *The English Journal* 85, no. 7 (1996): 15-24.

63 Weaver, Constance. "Teaching Grammar in the Context of Writing." *The English Journal* 85, no. 7 (1996): 15-24.

64 Mulroy, David. *The War Against Grammar*. Portsmouth, NH: Boynton/Cook Publishers, 2003, 60-61.

65 Mulroy, David. *The War Against Grammar*. Portsmouth, NH: Boynton/Cook Publishers, 2003, 62.

66 Mulroy, David. *The War Against Grammar*. Portsmouth, NH: Boynton/Cook Publishers, 2003, 64.

67 Mulroy, David. *The War Against Grammar*. Portsmouth, NH: Boynton/Cook Publishers, 2003.

68 Mulroy, David. *The War Against Grammar*. Portsmouth, NH: Boynton/Cook Publishers, 2003, 64.

69 Mulroy, David. *The War Against Grammar*. Portsmouth, NH: Boynton/Cook Publishers, 2003.

70 Blystone, Stephen M. "Caught in the Grammar Crossfire: One Student's Plea and Plan for Peace." *Issue in Writing* 12, no. 1 (2001): 24-42.

71 Mulroy, David. *The War Against Grammar*. Portsmouth, NH: Boynton/Cook Publishers, 2003, 74.

72 Mulroy, David. *The War Against Grammar*. Portsmouth, NH: Boynton/Cook Publishers, 2003, 6.

73 Mulroy, David. *The War Against Grammar*. Portsmouth, NH: Boynton/Cook Publishers, 2003, 74.

74 Mulroy, David. *The War Against Grammar*. Portsmouth, NH: Boynton/Cook Publishers, 2003, 7.

[75] Mulroy, David. *The War Against Grammar*. Portsmouth, NH: Boynton/Cook Publishers, 2003, 7.

[76] Hudson, Richard, and John Walmsley. "The English Patient: English Grammar and Teaching in the Twentieth Century." *Journal of Linguistics* 41, no. 3 (2005): 593-622.

[77] Mulroy, David. *The War Against Grammar*. Portsmouth, NH: Boynton/Cook Publishers, 2003, 13.

[78] Mulroy, David. *The War Against Grammar*. Portsmouth, NH: Boynton/Cook Publishers, 2003, 9.

[79] Mulroy, David. *The War Against Grammar*. Portsmouth, NH: Boynton/Cook Publishers, 2003, 9.

[80] Mulroy, David. *The War Against Grammar*. Portsmouth, NH: Boynton/Cook Publishers, 2003.

[81] Mulroy, David. *The War Against Grammar*. Portsmouth, NH: Boynton/Cook Publishers, 2003, 10.

[82] Mulroy, David. *The War Against Grammar*. Portsmouth, NH: Boynton/Cook Publishers, 2003, 14.

[83] Hudson, Richard, and John Walmsley. "The English Patient: English Grammar and Teaching in the Twentieth Century." *Journal of Linguistics* 41, no. 3 (2005): 593-622.

[84] Amare, Nicole. "Style: The New Grammar in Composition Studies?" In *Refiguring Prose Style: Possibilities for Writing Pedagogy*, edited by Theresa Johnson and Tom Pace, 153-66. University Press of Colorado, 2005. doi:10.2307/j.ctt4cgq34.17.

[85] Amare, Nicole. "Style: The New Grammar in Composition Studies?" In *Refiguring Prose Style: Possibilities for Writing Pedagogy*, edited by Theresa Johnson and Tom Pace, 153-66. University Press of Colorado, 2005. doi:10.2307/j.ctt4cgq34.17.

[86] Wardhaugh, Ronald. "If Grammar, Which Grammar, and How?" *College English* 29, no. 4 (1968): 303-09.

[87] Wardhaugh, Ronald. "If Grammar, Which Grammar, and How?" *College English* 29, no. 4 (1968): 303-09.

[88] Vavra, Ed. "On Not Teaching Grammar." *The English Journal* 85, no. 7 (1996): 32-37.

[89] Mulroy, David. *The War Against Grammar*. Portsmouth, NH: Boynton/Cook Publishers, 2003, 75.

[90] Roach, John, and Michael C. Thompson. "Personal Conversation with Michael Clay Thompson." February 18, 2019.

[91] Jones, Susan, Deborah Myhill, and Trevor Bailey. "Grammar for Writing? An Investigation of the Effects of Contextualized Grammar Teaching on Students' Writing." *Reading & Writing* 26, no. 8 (2012): 1241-63. doi:10.1007/s11145-012-9416-1.

[92] Jones, Susan, Deborah Myhill, and Trevor Bailey. "Grammar for Writing? An Investigation of the Effects of Contextualized Grammar Teaching on Students' Writing." *Reading & Writing* 26, no. 8 (2012): 1241-63. doi:10.1007/s11145-012-9416-1.

[93] Jones, Susan, Deborah Myhill, and Trevor Bailey. "Grammar for Writing? An Investigation of the Effects of Contextualized Grammar Teaching on Students' Writing." *Reading & Writing* 26, no. 8 (2012): 1241-63. doi:10.1007/s11145-012-9416-1.

[94] Singh, Ramjee. "Controversies in Teaching English Grammar." *Academic Voices: A Multi-disciplinary Journal* 1, no. 1 (2011): 56-60.

[95] Singh, Ramjee. "Controversies in Teaching English Grammar." *Academic Voices: A \Multi-disciplinary Journal* 1, no. 1 (2011): 56-60.

[96] Singh, Ramjee. "Controversies in Teaching English Grammar." *Academic Voices: A Multi-disciplinary Journal* 1, no. 1 (2011): 56-60.

[97] Nassaji, Hossein, and Sandra Fotos. "Current Developments in Research on the Teaching of Grammar." *Annual Review of Applied Linguistics* 24 (2004): 126-145.

[98] Mulroy, David. *The War Against Grammar*. Portsmouth, NH: Boynton/Cook Publishers, 2003, 66.

[99] Mulroy, David. *The War Against Grammar*. Portsmouth, NH: Boynton/Cook Publishers, 2003, 7.

[100] Mulroy, David. *The War Against Grammar*. Portsmouth, NH: Boynton/Cook Publishers, 2003, 7.

[101] English Language Arts Standards." *Common Core State Standards Initiative*, 2019.

[102] Mulroy, David. *The War Against Grammar*. Portsmouth, NH: Boynton/Cook Publishers, 2003, 7.

[103] Mulroy, David. *The War Against Grammar*. Portsmouth, NH: Boynton/Cook Publishers, 2003, 7.

[104] Singh, Ramjee. "Controversies in Teaching English Grammar." *Academic Voices: A Multi-disciplinary Journal* 1, no. 1 (2011): 56-60.

[105] Zhang, Jian. "Necessity of Grammar Teaching." *International Education Studies* 2, no. 2 (2009): 184-187. doi:10.5539/ies.v2n2p184.

[106] Mulroy, David. *The War Against Grammar*. Portsmouth, NH: Boynton/Cook Publishers, 2003.

[107] Mulroy, David. *The War Against Grammar*. Portsmouth, NH: Boynton/Cook Publishers, 2003, 4-5.

[108] Mulroy, David. *The War Against Grammar*. Portsmouth, NH: Boynton/Cook Publishers, 2003, 5.

[109] Mulroy, David. *The War Against Grammar*. Portsmouth, NH: Boynton/Cook Publishers, 2003, 66.

[110] Mulroy, David. *The War Against Grammar*. Portsmouth, NH: Boynton/Cook Publishers, 2003, 70-71.

[111] Mulroy, David. *The War Against Grammar*. Portsmouth, NH: Boynton/Cook Publishers, 2003, 6.

112 Mulroy, David. *The War Against Grammar*. Portsmouth, NH: Boynton/Cook Publishers, 2003.

113 Mulroy, David. *The War Against Grammar*. Portsmouth, NH: Boynton/Cook Publishers, 2003, 6.

114 Mulroy, David. *The War Against Grammar*. Portsmouth, NH: Boynton/Cook Publishers, 2003, 6.

115 Mulroy, David. *The War Against Grammar*. Portsmouth, NH: Boynton/Cook Publishers, 2003, 115.

116 Ravitch, Diane. "Subordinate Clause Without Any Pauses: Why We Need a Language With Some Lawses." *Education Next* 5, no. 2 (2005): 78-79.

117 Goldstein, Dana. "Why Kids Can›t Write." *The New York Times*, August 2, 2017.

118 Goldstein, Dana. "Why Kids Can›t Write." *The New York Times*, August 2, 2017.

119 Mulroy, David. *The War Against Grammar*. Portsmouth, NH: Boynton/Cook Publishers, 2003, 8.

120 Mulroy, David. *The War Against Grammar*. Portsmouth, NH: Boynton/Cook Publishers, 2003, 8.

121 Mulroy, David. *The War Against Grammar*. Portsmouth, NH: Boynton/Cook Publishers, 2003, 8.

122 Haussamen, Brock, et al. *Grammar Alive! A Guide for Teachers*. Urbana, IL: NCTE, 2002, 1.

123 Mulroy, David. *The War Against Grammar*. Portsmouth, NH: Boynton/Cook Publishers, 2003, 88.

124 Mulroy, David. *The War Against Grammar*. Portsmouth, NH: Boynton/Cook Publishers, 2003, 88.

125 Blystone, Stephen M. "Caught in the Grammar Crossfire: One Student's Plea and Plan for Peace." *Issue in Writing* 12, no. 1 (2001): 24-42.

126 Mulroy, David. *The War Against Grammar*. Portsmouth, NH: Boynton/Cook Publishers, 2003, 88.

127 Blystone, Stephen M. "Caught in the Grammar Crossfire: One Student's Plea and Plan for Peace." *Issue in Writing* 12, no. 1 (2001): 24-42.

128 Ravitch, Diane. "Subordinate Clause Without Any Pauses: Why We Need a Language With Some Lawses." *Education Next* 5, no. 2 (2005): 78-79.

129 Ravitch, Diane. "Subordinate Clause Without Any Pauses: Why We Need a Language With Some Lawses." *Education Next* 5, no. 2 (2005): 78-79.

130 Ravitch, Diane. "Subordinate Clause Without Any Pauses: Why We Need a Language With Some Lawses." *Education Next* 5, no. 2 (2005): 78-79.

131 Ravitch, Diane. "Subordinate Clause Without Any Pauses: Why We Need a Language With Some Lawses." *Education Next* 5, no. 2 (2005): 78-79.

132 Asselin, Marlene. "Teaching Grammar." *Teacher Librarian* 29, no. 5 (2002): 52-53.

133 Mulroy, David. *The War Against Grammar*. Portsmouth, NH: Boynton/Cook Publishers, 2003, 2.

134 Roach, John, and Michael C. Thompson. "Personal Conversation with Michael Clay Thompson." February 18, 2019.

135 Jones, Susan, Deborah Myhill, and Trevor Bailey. "Grammar for Writing? An Investigation of the Effects of Contextualized Grammar Teaching on Students' Writing." *Reading & Writing* 26, no. 8 (2012): 1241-1263. doi:10.1007/s11145-012-9416-1.

136 Jones, Susan, Deborah Myhill, and Trevor Bailey. "Grammar for Writing? An Investigation of the Effects of Contextualized Grammar Teaching on Students' Writing." *Reading & Writing* 26, no. 8 (2012): 1241-1263. doi:10.1007/s11145-012-9416-1.

137 Anderson, Jeff. *Mechanically Inclined: Building Grammar, Usage, and Style into Writers Workshop*. Portland, ME: Stenhouse Publishers, 2005, 14.

138 Anderson, Jeff. *Mechanically Inclined: Building Grammar, Usage, and Style into Writers Workshop*. Portland, ME: Stenhouse Publishers, 2005, 14.

139 Thompson, Michael C. *Advanced Academic Writing. Volume 2*. Unionville, NY: Royal Fireworks Press, 2009.

140 Jones, Susan, Deborah Myhill, and Trevor Bailey. "Grammar for Writing? An Investigation of the Effects of Contextualized Grammar Teaching on Students' Writing." *Reading & Writing* 26, no. 8 (2012): 1241-1263. doi:10.1007/s11145-012-9416-1.

141 Hudson, Richard, and John Walmsley. "The English Patient: English Grammar and Teaching in the Twentieth Century." *Journal of Linguistics* 41, no. 3 (2005): 593-622.

142 Zhang, Jian. "Necessity of Grammar Teaching." *International Education Studies* 2, no. 2 (2009): 184-187. doi:10.5539/ies.v2n2p184.

143 Sams, Laura. "How to Teach Grammar, Analytical Thinking, and Writing: A Method That Works." *The English Journal* 92, no. 3 (2003): 57-64.

144 Thompson, Michael C. *The Verbal Option*. Understanding Our Gifted 14, no. 1 (2001): 7-10.

145 Petruzzella, Barbara A. "Grammar Instruction: What Teachers Say." *The English Journal* 85, no. 7 (1996): 68-72.

146 Berger, John. "A Systematic Approach to Grammar Instruction." *Voices from the Middle* 8, no. 3 (2001): 43-49.

147 Berger, John. "A Systematic Approach to Grammar Instruction." *Voices from the Middle* 8, no. 3 (2001): 43-49.

148 Berger, John. "A Systematic Approach to Grammar Instruction." *Voices from the Middle* 8, no. 3 (2001): 43-49.

149 Berger, John. "A Systematic Approach to Grammar Instruction." *Voices from the Middle* 8, no. 3 (2001): 43-49.

150 Blasé, Dana, McFarlan, Robert, and Little, Sarah. "Bridging the Grammar Gap: An Interdisciplinary Approach." *The English Journal* 92, no. 3 (2003): 51-56. doi:10.2307/822260.

[151] Neuleib, Janice, and Brosnahan, Linda. "Teaching Grammar to Writers." *Journal of Basic Writing* 6, no. 1 (1987): 28-35.

[152] Sams, Laura. "How to Teach Grammar, Analytical Thinking, and Writing: A Method That Works." *The English Journal* 92, no. 3 (2003): 57-64.

[153] Buerke, Amanda M. "Relationship Between Traditional Grammar Terminology and Metacognitive Application of Grammar Concepts." *Master of Education Program Theses*, Dordt University, 2005, 17-18.

[154] Buerke, Amanda M. "Relationship Between Traditional Grammar Terminology and Metacognitive Application of Grammar Concepts." *Master of Education Program Theses*, Dordt University, 2005.

[155] Buerke, Amanda M. "Relationship Between Traditional Grammar Terminology and Metacognitive Application of Grammar Concepts." *Master of Education Program Theses*, Dordt University, 2005, 14.

[156] Buerke, Amanda M. "Relationship Between Traditional Grammar Terminology and Metacognitive Application of Grammar Concepts." *Master of Education Program Theses*, Dordt University, 2005, 11.

[157] Buerke, Amanda M. "Relationship Between Traditional Grammar Terminology and Metacognitive Application of Grammar Concepts." *Master of Education Program Theses*, Dordt University, 2005, 12.

[158] Blasé, Dana, McFarlan, Robert, and Little, Sarah. "Bridging the Grammar Gap: An Interdisciplinary Approach." *The English Journal* 92, no. 3 (2003): 51-56. doi:10.2307/822260.

[159] Weaver, Constance, McNally, Constance, and Moerman, Susan. "To Grammar or Not to Grammar: That Is Not the Question!" *Voices from the Middle* 8, no. 3 (2001): 17-33.

[160] Buerke, Amanda M. "Relationship Between Traditional Grammar Terminology and Metacognitive Application of Grammar Concepts." *Master of Education Program Theses*, Dordt University, 2005, 1.

[161] Asselin, Marlene. "Teaching Grammar." *Teacher Librarian* 29, no. 5 (2002): 52-53.

[162] Mulroy, David. *The War Against Grammar*. Portsmouth, NH: Boynton/Cook Publishers, 2003, 9.

[163] Singleton, Carl. "We Can Never Teach Students to Write If They Can't Use Standard Grammar." *Chronicle of Higher Education*, May 20, 1987, 40.

[164] Singleton, Carl. "We Can Never Teach Students to Write If They Can't Use Standard Grammar." *Chronicle of Higher Education*, May 20, 1987, 41.

[165] Singleton, Carl. "We Can Never Teach Students to Write If They Can't Use Standard Grammar." *Chronicle of Higher Education*, May 20, 1987, 41.

[166] Buerke, Amanda M. "Relationship Between Traditional Grammar Terminology and Metacognitive Application of Grammar Concepts." *Master of Education Program Theses*, Dordt University, 2005, 18.

[167] Buerke, Amanda M. "Relationship Between Traditional Grammar Terminology and Metacognitive Application of Grammar Concepts." *Master of Education Program Theses*, Dordt University, 2005.

[168] Thompson, Michael C. *Vocabulary and Grammar: Critical Content for Critical Thinking. Journal of Secondary Gifted Education* 13, no. 2 (2002): 60-66.

[169] Anderson, Jeff. *Mechanically Inclined: Building Grammar, Usage, and Style into Writers Workshop*. Portland, ME: Stenhouse Publishers, 2005, 13.

[170] Ravitch, Diane. "Subordinate Clause Without Any Pauses: Why We Need a Language With Some Lawses." *Education Next* 5, no. 2 (2005): 78-79.

[171] Mulroy, David. *The War Against Grammar*. Portsmouth, NH: Boynton/Cook Publishers, 2003, 87.

[172] Ravitch, Diane. "Subordinate Clause Without Any Pauses: Why We Need a Language With Some Lawses." *Education Next* 5, no. 2 (2005): 78-79.

[173] LaChance, Michelle. "English Dept. at Rutgers to Deemphasize Traditional Grammar in Solidarity With Black Lives Matter." *Legal Insurrection*, July 24, 2020.

[174] LaChance, Michelle. "English Dept. at Rutgers to Deemphasize Traditional Grammar in Solidarity With Black Lives Matter." *Legal Insurrection*, July 24, 2020.

[175] LaChance, Michelle. "English Dept. at Rutgers to Deemphasize Traditional Grammar in Solidarity With Black Lives Matter." *Legal Insurrection*, July 24, 2020.

[176] LaChance, Michelle. "English Dept. at Rutgers to Deemphasize Traditional Grammar in Solidarity With Black Lives Matter." *Legal Insurrection*, July 24, 2020.

[177] "Stagepost Live Shot Guests." Carol Swain - Fox News, July 23, 2020. YouTube. https://www.youtube.com/watch?v=JoYs6G-Wqlo.

[178] "Stagepost Live Shot Guests." Carol Swain - Fox News, July 23, 2020. YouTube. https://www.youtube.com/watch?v=JoYs6G-Wqlo.

[179] "Stagepost Live Shot Guests." Carol Swain - Fox News, July 23, 2020. YouTube.https://www.youtube.com/watch?v=JoYs6G-Wqlo.

[180] "Stagepost Live Shot Guests." Carol Swain - Fox News, July 23, 2020. YouTube.https://www.youtube.com/watch?v=JoYs6G-Wqlo.

[181] Mulroy, David. *The War Against Grammar*. Portsmouth, NH: Boynton/Cook Publishers, 2003.

[182] Mulroy, David. *The War Against Grammar*. Portsmouth, NH: Boynton/Cook Publishers, 2003, 79.

[183] Mulroy, David. *The War Against Grammar*. Portsmouth, NH: Boynton/Cook Publishers, 2003, 87-88.

[184] Mulroy, David. *The War Against Grammar*. Portsmouth, NH: Boynton/Cook Publishers, 2003, 79.

185 Mulroy, David. *The War Against Grammar*. Portsmouth, NH: Boynton/Cook Publishers, 2003.

186 Mulroy, David. *The War Against Grammar*. Portsmouth, NH: Boynton/Cook Publishers, 2003, 118.

187 Oldenburg, Scott. "Grammar in the Student-Centered Composition Class." *Radical Teacher: A Socialist, Feminist, and Anti-Racist Journal on the Theory and Practice of Teaching* 75 (2006): 56-57.

188 Adoniou, Misty. "Grammar Matters and Should Be Taught—Differently." *The Conversation*, April 16, 2014. https://theconversation.com/grammar-matters-and-should-be-taught-differently-25604.

189 Adoniou, Misty. "Grammar Matters and Should Be Taught—Differently." *The Conversation*, April 16, 2014. https://theconversation.com/grammar-matters-and-should-be-taught-differently-25604.

190 Howe, Wayne A., and Penelope Lisi. *Becoming a Multicultural Educator: Developing Awareness, Gaining Skills, and Taking Action*. Thousand Oaks, CA: SAGE Publications

191 Gay, Geneva. "Preparing for Culturally Responsive Teaching." *Journal of Teacher Education* 53, no. 2 (2002): 106-116.

192 Thompson, Michael C. *The Magic Lens*. Vol. 2. Unionville, NY: Royal Fireworks Press, 2002, iv.

193 Thompson, Michael C. *The Magic Lens*. Vol. 2. Unionville, NY: Royal Fireworks Press, 2002, iv.

194 Jones, Susan, Deborah Myhill, and Trevor Bailey. "Grammar for Writing? An Investigation of the Effects of Contextualized Grammar Teaching on Students' Writing." *Reading & Writing* 26, no. 8 (2012): 1241-1263. doi:10.1007/s11145-012-9416-1.

195 Vavra, Ed. "On Not Teaching Grammar." *The English Journal* 85, no. 7 (1996): 32-37.

196 "Effective Grammar Instruction." *YourDictionary*. Accessed February 17, 2019. https://education.yourdictionary.com/for-teachers/effective-grammar-instruction.html.

197 "Effective Grammar Instruction." *YourDictionary*. Accessed February 17, 2019.https://education.yourdictionary.com/for-teachers/effective-grammar-instruction.html.

198 Mulroy, David. *The War Against Grammar*. Portsmouth, NH: Boynton/Cook Publishers, 2003, 75.

199 Mulroy, David. *The War Against Grammar*. Portsmouth, NH: Boynton/Cook Publishers, 2003, 79.

200 Zhang, Jian. "Necessity of Grammar Teaching." *International Education Studies* 2, no. 2 (2009): 184-187. doi:10.5539/ies.v2n2p184.

201 Zhang, Jian. "Necessity of Grammar Teaching." *International Education Studies* 2, no. 2 (2009): 184-187. doi:10.5539/ies.v2n2p184.

202 Thompson, Michael C. *The Magic Lens*. Vol. 2. Unionville, NY: Royal Fireworks Press, 2002, v.

[203] Hudson, Richard, and John Walmsley. "The English Patient: English Grammar and Teaching in the Twentieth Century." *Journal of Linguistics* 41, no. 3 (2005): 593-622.

[204] Nassaji, Hossein, and Sandra Fotos. "Current Developments in Research on the Teaching of Grammar." *Annual Review of Applied Linguistics* 24 (2004): 126-145.

[205] Azar, Betty Schrampfer. "Grammar Teaching and Communicative Teaching: A Hybrid That Works." Paper presented at TESOL 2008: "Teaching Grammar in Today's Classroom," February 15, 2019. www.azargrammar.com.

[206] Azar, Betty Schrampfer. "Grammar Teaching and Communicative Teaching: A Hybrid That Works." Paper presented at TESOL 2008: "Teaching Grammar in Today's Classroom," February 15, 2019. www.azargrammar.com.

[207] Lin, Lin. "The Role of Grammar Teaching in Writing in Second Language Acquisition. *ERIC*, November 12, 2008. https://eric.ed.gov/?id=ED503439.

[208] Thompson, Michael C. *The Verbal Option*. Understanding Our Gifted 14, no. 1 (2001): 7-10.[209] Sams, Laura. "How to Teach Grammar, Analytical Thinking, and Writing: A Method That Works." *The English Journal* 92, no. 3 (2003): 57-64.

[210] Mulroy, David. *The War Against Grammar*. Portsmouth, NH: Boynton/Cook Publishers, 2003, xi.

[211] Mulroy, David. *The War Against Grammar*. Portsmouth, NH: Boynton/Cook Publishers, 2003, 3.

[212] Azar, Betty Schrampfer. "Grammar Teaching and Communicative Teaching: A Hybrid That Works." Paper presented at TESOL 2008: "Teaching Grammar in Today's Classroom," February 15, 2019. www.azargrammar.com.

[213] Sams, Laura. "How to Teach Grammar, Analytical Thinking, and Writing: A Method That Works." *The English Journal* 92, no. 3 (2003): 57-64.

[214] Vavra, Ed. "On Not Teaching Grammar." *The English Journal* 85, no. 7 (1996): 32-37.

[215] Roach, John, and Michael C. Thompson. "Personal Conversation with Michael Clay Thompson." February 18, 2019.

[216] Johnson, Andrew P. *Academic Writing: Process and Product*. Lanham, MD: Rowman & Littlefield, 2016.

[217] Vavra, Ed. "On Not Teaching Grammar." *The English Journal* 85, no. 7 (1996): 32-37.

[218] Berger, John. "A Systematic Approach to Grammar Instruction." *Voices from the Middle* 8, no. 3 (2001): 43-49.

[219] Thompson, Michael C. *Four-Level Grammar and Academic Writing*. Unionville, NY: Royal Fireworks Press, n.d., 9.

[220] Johnson, Andrew P. *Academic Writing: Process and Product*. Lanham, MD: Rowman & Littlefield, 2016, 99.

[221] Thompson, Michael C. *Advanced Academic Writing. Volume 2*. Unionville, NY: Royal Fireworks Press, 2009.

[222] Thompson, Michael C. *The Magic Lens*. Vol. 2. Unionville, NY: Royal Fireworks Press, 2002, v.

[223] Thompson, Michael C. *The Magic Lens*. Vol. 2. Unionville, NY: Royal Fireworks Press, 2002.

[224] Thompson, Michael C. *Four-Level Grammar and Academic Writing*. Unionville, NY: Royal Fireworks Press, n.d., 9.

[225] Roach, John, and Michael C. Thompson. "Personal Conversation with Michael Clay Thompson." February 18, 2019.

[226] Anderson, Jeff. *Mechanically Inclined: Building Grammar, Usage, and Style into Writers Workshop*. Portland, ME: Stenhouse Publishers, 2005, xii.

[227] Truss, Lynne. *Eats, Shoots & Leaves: The Zero Tolerance Approach to Punctuation*. New York, NY: Gotham Books, 2003, 202.

[228] Thompson, Michael C. *The Magic Lens*. Vol. 2. Unionville, NY: Royal Fireworks Press, 2002, iv.

[229] Haussamen, Brock, et al. *Grammar Alive! A Guide for Teachers*. Urbana, IL: NCTE, 2002, 2.

[230] Johnson, Andrew P. *Academic Writing: Process and Product*. Lanham, MD: Rowman & Littlefield, 2016, xii.

[231] Mulroy, David. *The War Against Grammar*. Portsmouth, NH: Boynton/Cook Publishers, 2003, 22.

[232] Hudson, Richard, and John Walmsley. "The English Patient: English Grammar and Teaching in the Twentieth Century." *Journal of Linguistics* 41, no. 3 (2005): 593-622.

[233] Ravitch, Diane. "Subordinate Clause Without Any Pauses: Why We Need a Language With Some Lawses." *Education Next* 5, no. 2 (2005): 78-79.

[234] Hudson, Richard, and John Walmsley. "The English Patient: English Grammar and Teaching in the Twentieth Century." *Journal of Linguistics* 41, no. 3 (2005): 593-622.

[235] Mulroy, David. *The War Against Grammar*. Portsmouth, NH: Boynton/Cook Publishers, 2003, 104.

[236] Mulroy, David. *The War Against Grammar*. Portsmouth, NH: Boynton/Cook Publishers, 2003, 104.

[237] Jones, Susan, Deborah Myhill, and Trevor Bailey. "Grammar for Writing? An Investigation of the Effects of Contextualized Grammar Teaching on Students' Writing." *Reading & Writing* 26, no. 8 (2012): 1241-1263. doi:10.1007/s11145-012-9416-1.

[238] Mulroy, David. *The War Against Grammar*. Portsmouth, NH: Boynton/Cook Publishers, 2003, 5.

[239] Roach, John, and Michael C. Thompson. "Personal Conversation with Michael Clay Thompson." February 18, 2019.

240 Adoniou, Misty. "Grammar Matters and Should Be Taught—Differently." *The Conversation*, April 16, 2014. https://theconversation.com/grammar-matters-and-should-be-taught-differently-25604.

241 Vavra, Ed. "On Not Teaching Grammar." *The English Journal* 85, no. 7 (1996): 36.

242 Asselin, Marlene. "Teaching Grammar." *Teacher Librarian* 29, no. 5 (2002): 52-53.

243 Adoniou, Misty. "Exemplary Literature and Grammar Instruction. *The Conversation*, April 16, 2014. https://theconversation.com/grammar-matters-and-should-be-taught-differently-25604.

244 Adoniou, Misty. "Exemplary Literature and Grammar Instruction. *The Conversation*, April 16, 2014. https://theconversation.com/grammar-matters-and-should-be-taught-differently-25604.

245 Sams, Laura. "The Writing Process and Idea Development." *The English Journal* 92, no. 3 (2003): 58.

246 Sams, Laura. "The Writing Process and Idea Development." *The English Journal* 92, no. 3 (2003): 58.

247 Benjamin, Amy, et al. *The Assembly for the Teaching of English Grammar Resolution: On the Value of Systematic Grammar Study*. Accessed June 24, 2019. https://ateg.weebly.com/uploads/1/5/9/4/15949950/on_the_value_of_systematic_grammar_study.pdf

248 Benjamin, Amy, et al. *The Assembly for the Teaching of English Grammar Resolution: On the Value of Systematic Grammar Study*. Accessed June 24, 2019. https://ateg.weebly.com/uploads/1/5/9/4/15949950/on_the_value_of_systematic_grammar_study.pdf

249 Benjamin, Amy, et al. *The Assembly for the Teaching of English Grammar Resolution: On the Value of Systematic Grammar Study*. Accessed June 24, 2019. https://ateg.weebly.com/uploads/1/5/9/4/15949950/on_the_value_of_systematic_grammar_study.pdf

250 Michael Clay Thompson: Biography." Accessed February 19, 2019. https://www.rfwp.com/pages/michael-clay-thompson/biography/.

251 "Michael Clay Thompson: Biography." Accessed February 19, 2019. https://www.rfwp.com/pages/michael-clay-thompson/biography/.

252 Thompson, Michael C. *Grammar Voyage*. Unionville, NY: Royal Fireworks Press, 2012.

253 Sams, Laura. "How to Teach Grammar, Analytical Thinking, and Writing: A Method That Works." *The English Journal* 92, no. 3 (2003): 62.

254 Sams, Laura. "How to Teach Grammar, Analytical Thinking, and Writing: A Method That Works." *The English Journal* 92, no. 3 (2003): 62.

255 Vavra, Ed. "On Not Teaching Grammar." *The English Journal* 85, no. 7 (1996): 34.

256 Vavra, Ed. "On Not Teaching Grammar." *The English Journal* 85, no. 7 (1996): 35.

257 Weaver, Constance, McNally, Constance, and Moerman, Susan. "To Grammar or Not to Grammar: That Is Not the Question!" *Voices from the Middle* 8, no. 3 (2001): 17-33.

[258] Sams, Laura. "How to Teach Grammar, Analytical Thinking, and Writing: A Method That Works." *The English Journal* 92, no. 3 (2003): 57.

[259] Berger, John. "A Systematic Approach to Grammar Instruction." *Voices from the Middle* 8, no. 3 (2001): 47.

[260] Berger, John. "A Systematic Approach to Grammar Instruction." *Voices from the Middle* 8, no. 3 (2001): 48.

[261] Berger, John. "A Systematic Approach to Grammar Instruction." *Voices from the Middle* 8, no. 3 (2001): 49.

[262] Blasé, Dana, McFarlan, Robert, and Little, Sarah. "Bridging the Grammar Gap: An Interdisciplinary Approach." *The English Journal* 92, no. 3 (2003): 51-56. doi:10.2307/822260.

[263] Nassaji, Hossein, and Sandra Fotos. "Current Developments in Research on the Teaching of Grammar." *Annual Review of Applied Linguistics* 24 (2004): 126-145.

[264] Nassaji, Hossein, and Sandra Fotos. "Current Developments in Research on the Teaching of Grammar." *Annual Review of Applied Linguistics* 24 (2004): 126-145.

[265] Sams, Laura. "How to Teach Grammar, Analytical Thinking, and Writing: A Method That Works." *The English Journal* 92, no. 3 (2003): 59.

[266] Sams, Laura. "How to Teach Grammar, Analytical Thinking, and Writing: A Method That Works." *The English Journal* 92, no. 3 (2003): 59.

[267] Sams, Laura. "How to Teach Grammar, Analytical Thinking, and Writing: A Method That Works." *The English Journal* 92, no. 3 (2003): 59.

[268] Blystone, Stephen M. "Caught in the Grammar Crossfire: One Student's Plea and Plan for Peace." *Issue in Writing* 12, no. 1 (2001): 24-42.

[269] Thompson, Michael C. *Four-Level Sentence Analysis.* Unionville, NY: Royal Fireworks Press, 2017, 2.

[270] Thompson, Michael C. *Four-Level Sentence Analysis.* Unionville, NY: Royal Fireworks Press, 2017, 2.

[271] Thompson, Michael C. *Four-Level Sentence Analysis.* Unionville, NY: Royal Fireworks Press, 2017, 3.

[272] Thompson, Michael C. *Four-Level Grammar and Academic Writing.* Unionville, NY: Royal Fireworks Press, n.d., 9.

[273] Vavra, Ed. "Grammar Through Inquiry." *The English Journal* 85, no. 7 (1996): 32-37.

[274] Neuleib, Janice, and Linda Brosnahan. "Teaching Grammar to Writers." *Journal of Basic Writing* 6, no. 1 (1987): 28-35.

[275] Adoniou, Misty. "Exemplary Literature and Grammar Instruction." *The Conversation*, April 16, 2014. https://theconversation.com/grammar-matters-and-should-be-taught-differently-25604.

[276] Vavra, Ed. "Grammar Through Inquiry." *The English Journal* 85, no. 7 (1996): 34.

[277] Haussamen, Brock, et al. *Grammar Alive! A Guide for Teachers.* Urbana, IL: NCTE, 2002, 3.

[278] Singleton, Carl. "We Can Never Teach Students to Write If They Can't Use Standard Grammar." *Chronicle of Higher Education*, May 20, 1987, 1.

[279] Vavra, Ed. "Grammar as Inquiry." *The English Journal* 85, no. 7 (1996): 37.

[280] Adoniou, Misty. "Creativity and Grammar Instruction." *The Conversation*, April 16, 2014. https://theconversation.com/grammar-matters-and-should-be-taught-differently-25604.

[281] Adoniou, Misty. "Creativity and Grammar Instruction." *The Conversation*, April 16, 2014.

[282] Adoniou, Misty. "The Decline of Grammar Teaching." *The Conversation*, April 16, 2014, 4.

[283] Sams, Laura. "The Writing Process and Idea Development." *The English Journal* 92, no. 3 (2003): 58.

[284] Sams, Laura. "How to Teach Grammar, Analytical Thinking, and Writing: A Method That Works." *The English Journal* 92, no. 3 (2003): 64.

About the Author

Jennifer Roach, Ed.D., holds a Bachelor of Arts in English from Virginia Commonwealth University, a Master of Arts in Teaching from Clemson University, a Specialist in Education in Educational Leadership from Arkansas State University, and a Doctorate of Education in Professional Leadership from Converse University. Her dissertation entitled "The Effect of Systematic Grammar Instruction on Academic Writing Ability," successfully defended to the Graduate School of Converse University in May of 2021, was given the "Dr. Thomas McDaniel Outstanding Dissertation Award." This honor is awarded to the graduate whose dissertation is judged to be the most potentially influential by having the most far-reaching implications for professional leadership in the context of education. Dr. Roach has over seventeen years of experience in education as both a teacher and administrator and is currently the Principal of Riverside Middle School in Pendleton, South Carolina.

Book Study Discussion Questions

Chapter 1

1. What are the main reasons the anti-grammar movement gained traction in education, and how have these reasons affected your approach to teaching grammar?
2. How do conflicting viewpoints on grammar instruction between educators and researchers create challenges for you as a teacher?
3. What role does socioeconomic background play in students' ability to "pick up" grammar through exposure to good writing, and how can systematic grammar instruction help bridge this gap?
4. In your experience, how effective is teaching grammar in the context of student writing versus direct instruction in isolation? Can these approaches complement each other?
5. How might faulty research from the 1960s and 1970s have influenced current educational policies regarding grammar, and how can teachers critically evaluate such research?
6. What impact does the decline in American literacy and academic writing ability have on students' future success in college and the workplace?
7. What do your current state standards say about teaching grammar, and how has this changed over time?
8. How can systematic grammar instruction be reframed to make it engaging and relevant for students, rather than being viewed as tedious or unnecessary?
9. How do you respond to mixed messages from different leadership levels regarding the teaching of grammar in your own classroom practices?
10. How can grammar instruction be seen as an essential part of critical thinking and intellectual development, and how might this view influence your teaching practices?

Chapter 2

1. How has the historical understanding of grammar as an academic discipline influenced your perspective on its importance in modern education?
2. What can be learned from the decline in literacy and writing proficiency since the 1960s when grammar instruction was minimized in schools?
3. How do you balance the progressive education approach that emphasizes creativity and student choice with the need for formal grammar instruction?
4. Considering the historical role of grammar in shaping critical thinking and intellectual development, how can we reintegrate systematic grammar teaching without reverting to outdated, tedious methods?
5. How might political and cultural factors, such as those mentioned by Constance Weaver, have contributed to the de-emphasis of grammar teaching? Do you see similar factors at play today?
6. What are the potential long-term effects on students' academic and professional success if grammar continues to be taught in a limited or inconsistent manner?
7. In your experience, how has the historical shift from traditional grammar instruction to progressive methods impacted students' writing and communication skills?
8. Given the resurgence of interest in grammar teaching, what strategies or methods can you implement in your classroom to make grammar instruction more engaging and effective?
9. What role should educational organizations like the NCTE and ATEG play in shaping the future of grammar instruction in schools?
10. How can technology and modern resources, like websites and digital tools, be used to enhance grammar instruction, making it more accessible and less "boring" for students?

Chapter 3

1. How do you see the divide between public opinion and academia regarding grammar instruction playing out in your school or district?
2. How do current trends, such as teaching grammar only in the context of student writing, impact your ability to help students master grammatical concepts?
3. What role do you think teacher confidence in their own grammar knowledge plays in how effectively grammar is taught today, and how can this be improved?
4. How do you respond to the argument that grammar instruction is oppressive or devalues cultural dialects? Is it possible to teach standard grammar while being culturally responsive?
5. What challenges do you face in balancing the expectations of teaching creativity in writing with the need to ensure grammatical accuracy?
6. How can you reconcile the time constraints of individual student conferencing or writing workshops with the need for systematic grammar instruction?
7. In what ways does the use of metaphorical terminology in place of academic grammar vocabulary create barriers to student understanding?
8. What steps can be taken to ensure grammar instruction is relevant, engaging, and integrated into writing without sacrificing the necessary depth of understanding?
9. How can grammar instruction be adapted to meet the needs of students from diverse linguistic backgrounds while maintaining high academic standards?
10. What are some ways you can incorporate both direct, systematic grammar instruction and writing workshops to create a balanced approach in your classroom?

Chapter 4

1. How does teaching grammar as a method of critical thinking and metacognition influence students' overall writing abilities?
2. What are the challenges and benefits of helping students move from declarative knowledge (knowing grammar rules) to procedural knowledge (applying grammar in writing)?
3. How can the idea of "growth through struggle" in grammar instruction help students develop resilience and persistence in writing?
4. In what ways can teaching students both prescriptive grammar rules and the evolving nature of language empower them to write more creatively and academically?
5. How does systematic grammar instruction support students' ability to engage in both creative and academic writing, and how do you balance these two forms in your classroom?
6. How can a strong foundation in grammar improve students' performance in other writing domains, such as sentence fluency, organization, and word choice?
7. What is the connection between understanding grammatical structures and improving students' abilities to read and comprehend complex texts, such as Shakespeare or academic literature?
8. How does teaching grammar enhance students' success in foreign language study and support English language learners in their mastery of English?
9. What strategies can you implement to move beyond error correction in grammar teaching and help students use grammar to enhance their writing's voice, style, and clarity?
10. How does understanding punctuation as a function of grammar give students more control over the meaning and impact of their writing?

Chapter 5

1. What lessons can be drawn from England's "rebirth of grammar teaching," and how can these reforms inform grammar instruction in American classrooms?
2. How do you think the curriculum standards movement, including the Common Core, has influenced the teaching of grammar in your school or district? What more needs to be done?
3. In your experience, how well-prepared are new teachers to teach grammar, and how might teacher preparation programs improve to address gaps in grammar instruction?
4. What are some of the challenges and benefits of implementing vertical planning for systematic grammar instruction from kindergarten through 12th grade?
5. How can the four levels of grammar (parts of speech, parts of the sentence, phrases, and clauses) be incorporated into your teaching to help students understand the structure of the English language?
6. What role should classroom action research by experienced teachers play in shaping future educational practices related to grammar teaching? How can their voices be more widely heard?

Chapter 6

1. How does the analogy of grammar being like "breathing in" and writing like "breathing out" shape your understanding of the connection between grammar instruction and writing?
2. How can teachers best use a Writing Workshop structure in a 60-minute or 90-minute class period to ensure that all students receive individualized support while still progressing through the writing process?
3. Why do you think narrative writing is recommended as the focus for the first nine weeks of the school year, and how can this help build student confidence as writers?
4. What are the benefits of teaching writing in specific units, such as narrative, informational, argumentative, and literary analysis, while reinforcing grammar skills throughout?
5. How can mini-lessons be designed to focus on key writing skills (such as crafting a thesis or organizing an essay) while reinforcing grammar concepts?
6. In what ways can conferencing with students during the Writing Workshop enhance their growth as writers, and how can teachers effectively manage time to ensure all students receive feedback?
7. What challenges might teachers face when integrating systematic grammar instruction into writing lessons, and how can they overcome these challenges?
8. How can teachers effectively incorporate technology, such as artificial intelligence tools like ChatGPT, to assist students in the revising and editing process while still maintaining students' voice and originality?
9. What strategies can be used to ensure that students understand the difference between revising for content and editing for grammar and conventions, and why is this distinction important?
10. How can teachers modernize their resources and avoid relying solely on skill-and-drill methods when teaching grammar, making it more engaging for students?

Please scan for additional materials

www.ingramcontent.com/pod-product-compliance
Lightning Source LLC
Chambersburg PA
CBHW080912280325
24216CB00001B/4

* 9 7 8 1 9 5 3 3 6 0 3 5 9 *